AF338705

Context and Intimacy

New York, NY
United States of America
© 2025 Baruch Menache
All rights reserved.
Published by McWest & Associates
ISBN: 978-1-971928-26-5

Context and Intimacy

The Psychological Frameworks that Govern Human Connection

Baruch Menache

Part 1: Context

Exposition of Information and Psychological Boundaries

This book explores the interplay between two fundamental social experiences: context and intimacy. "Context" refers to the social, cultural, and psychological conditions that shape perception and interaction, while "intimacy" is the quality of closeness that allows individuals to be biologically grounded.

Without contextual material there is no opportunity for intimacy, as intimacy ascends only when an over-exposition of contextual material has not been grounded into the biological system. In the case of the vagabond, the instant surplus contextual material emerges, it is grounded in momentary biological need, which is extremely important to their daily living. In the non-vagabond life, biological needs are often unmet, and thus contextual excess can occur and subsequently without being grounded in current biological activity.

However, since this process does not account for the entirety of conscious exposition, only the mere necessity that proves an experience, it becomes an external sense of biological integration. The choice of intimacy will seek out the nearest conceptual material without any filter regarding its importance or sense of goodness.

Information that is exposed to the psyche may not occur naturally and is bound to certain pretexts that either allow or halt specific material. At the far end of the spectrum is unanimous exposure, which enters with such force and veracity that the psyche cannot manage, attend to, or filter the material. We must be careful with the term manage, as it implies a construct of the psyche, not a biological impediment of the physical system upon which the psyche runs.

Theoretically, the psyche can manage any degree of information, though it is constrained by physical limitations. The psyche can be viewed as software embedded within the hardware of the brain. Unlike computer software, however, its mainframe arises from the hardware itself, a topic for another occasion.

When too much information is presented at once, especially when it comes suddenly rather than through gradual interaction, it imprints directly on the psyche. There is no time for the mind to help process or resist it. At the other end of the spectrum we find material that surrounds perception but is not digested as a cognitive thread. The deliberateness of information, due to a lack of relativity or relevance, will be absorbed without any degree of attention, as if it were above or below the psyche.

While a large amount of attended informational material can deeply affect a person, the natural psyche does not require focused attention to absorb information, it takes in whatever surrounds it. There is a space between the psyche and material inhabited by elements whose sole purpose is to gauge the information exposition. Without these elements, the psyche would absorb everything to its full capacity. The first meeting between psyche and perceptual material will yield a very large degree of that capacity; subsequent exposures will yield less, eventually leading to a point where new material is barely absorbed.

The way the psyche manages the present is based on its memory of potent engagements. Even if new material engages only a small portion of the psyche's capacity, it will be laid upon former material and become subordinate to it. Thus, new information will always be old information, its newness only constructed from prior material upon which it is projected.

These pretexts govern the distribution of information exposition. While they decide what should be exposed to the psyche, they do not decide what should not be. Informational material surrounds the psyche and only enters based on these pretexts. If it has entered, we can assume it did so under a pretext. Even though pretexts control the exposition of information, we must grant that the present ones are themselves preceded by earlier pretexts. There is a point at which no pretext exists; yet once that moment has passed, an individual's life begins to absorb information through pretexts.

There are mechanisms that can remove pretexts, allowing the psyche to absorb information with a higher degree of capacity. This state is what we will call intimacy, defined here as a profound psychic openness where normal boundaries and filters are suspended. A child is intimately attached to the mother because she occupies a high capacity within the psyche. Anyone or anything can be an object of intimacy if it occupies a large portion of that capacity. Intimacy is the availability for a higher degree of information exposition, an exposition technically controlled by pretexts, which are removed at the moment of intimacy. We can view pretexts as the normative state of the psyche, seeking to run systems at optimal levels. Intimacy is the non-normative state, disrupting exposition to allow for undeterred exposure at any degree.

There is no protection within intimacy to control exposition, and there is always a risk of a heightened information load that the psyche cannot manage. When this occurs, the psyche is disrupted by a traumatic imprint, which engages a high capacity and acts as a major pretext in future life dealings.

When cognitive control of information exposition is exercised in the present moment, it uses a pretext to dispel an older one, this is considered a conflict in the interior of the psyche. Pretexts can be divided into two main categories (though fundamentally they may be one): context and intimacy. Context is a domain of informational material that naturally seeks to expand into the present. Intimacy is the depth of experience toward the material, typically based on a preceding context.

We can experience a certain context without engaging in intimacy, as not all information relates to layers of personhood. A context can be entertained without a conscious relationship to the psyche. Although all information is ultimately related to the psyche, this connection is not always consciously recognized. However, while all contexts relate to the psyche, some relate to more aspects of selfhood than others. This is the experienced intimacy of a context.

While intimacy may sometimes appear to arise without a preconceived context, closer reflection reveals that some latent context, however subtle, is always present. Whenever intimacy arises, we can unearth the contextual strands that caused it. We can also identify the relational material responsible for that depth of intimacy in terms of the extensive psyche.

This disjunction between an assumed reality and contextual discord creates conflict with the surrounding collective body. One who holds an assumed context of reality, set against the backdrop of another, will be in contention with others or elements within that social body or environment, especially if they are compelled to partake in that context, thereby losing the comfort of their own state of consciousness. This tension would constitute the most successful headway in a particular domain, emerging from slight friction due to their respective developments in consciousness.

Context as the Mediator

Context, as used here, refers to the situational frameworks, social, cultural, and psychological conditions, that mediate and shape perception. It serves as the bridge between the self and external reality. Every connecting element contains some version of context within it, and it is up to us to discern the framework of that bridge. One might call it the "reason" for the connection, framing the structure for relaying and reciprocating information. Yet, calling it simply "the reason" feels too vague. It remains embedded, distant from the actual relationship. In contrast, "context" emphasizes its role as an active information relay. As such, it constitutes the majority of the relationship itself.

With the utmost amount of context, almost the entirety of the information relay falls under the strict parameters of the contextual layer, such that nothing is shared, even if evidential, unless it is in relation to the contextual layer itself. Context is a separate relationship that mediates two parts of a relationship. It is the third-party that provides both a degree of separation and possibility of earnest interaction.

Within a relationship, there are many layers of context, so that the essence of the relationship may not be apparent to both proponents. The various contexts mediate the proponent, resulting in an eventual information relay that differs significantly from the raw contents of the relationship. However, one maintains a relationship to these contextual layers, which may include additional contexts. In this way, a context may supersede a contextual layer, which in turn supersedes the relationship itself.

The relationship cannot be completely raw; that would resemble the earliest stages of infancy, when no information relay exists, only an assumed center of selfhood represented by the Mother. The infant learns about the mother only by separation; the mother's knowledge is not inherited. This is because the infant is not innately the Mother and does not possess the mother's characterological tools for receiving information in the same way. The infant's learning begins in separation from the Mother, allowing the first contextual layers to form, making genuine connection and information exchange possible.

The context for a given context, what may be called secondary context, is of a different character than true context. Secondary context appears more accessible because it seems arbitrary, as it serves to protect the protection itself. We can approach the raw relationship of context more easily than we can approach an absolute relationship, since secondary context carries less risk of problematic outcomes, the very outcomes that all context seeks to guard against. When the relationship is of high degree, or when the connection is more intimate in its informational content, a more substantial contextual layer becomes necessary.

Contextual Bridge and Formation of Centers

When there are multiple centers, all within the range of a psyche's habitat, one relies more heavily on the conceptual realm and the context that connects them. When a person moves to a new political or geographical environment different from childhood, they become detached from their original center. Therefore, all perspectives in that environment will require a specific context. In a social form, this might be: "Why are you here?" In a psychological state, it could be: "How does this relate?" One will always contrast, not because they are born to be conceptual builders, like scientists studying contrast and intellectual matters, but because they have no other choice but to reckon with the current habitat as a mere example of interaction with the source of the environment.

Yet, one contains many forms of centers, and another could be familial attachment. In this way, one may alleviate the contextual burden by inquiring into and following other central realms, which will compensate in the meantime. These will create a buffer, for instance, a familial bond will help one endure by serving as another center, tethering them into another psycho-political system. The more distant the central realms, the more one is contextually bound, as they must find a bridge to all these centers. Without one's family in close proximity, they will begin to measure new relationships against the family framework, marking friendship in a more conceptual domain.

If one does not adhere to the contextual bridge of these centers, one becomes detached from their source and its prospective actualizations. One who fails to apply a contextual setting to current relationships, in relation to that source material, begins to lose attachment to those centers. They become lost in a new realm that does not establish itself as an entity, relying solely on a former actualization to interpret the current one. Without allowing that prior experience to inform their perspective, they remain stranded, with no vitality in their network of psychic connections.

Another issue arises when the non-vitalized center functions as a constant mechanism of interaction, but only subconsciously. In this case, all one's actions, particularly in relationships, are complete interactions with the prior center, not as development, but as repetition of what memory presumes that prior experience to have been. This happens because the repressed vitality of the center becomes a major preoccupation of the psyche, not in its nuances, but in the mere allowance for it to be experienced as it was. At the very least, the psyche justifies this by assuming there will be a revitalization of that memory, even if it remains infantile in nature. A realized prior-center is always deemed more important than a promising conceptual link to that same center.

With this understanding, we can explore the creation of a new center. By serving as a conceptual link, and thus as a contrast, the current relationship fosters constant interaction with the prior center from a new vantage point. This process gradually alleviates the vitality of the prior center until it almost vanishes. In this way, one becomes available to create a new center, built through a contextual mainframe.

In cases of geographical or political change, although contrast is always present, it rarely carries the weight of a newfound center, even if it provides contextual oversight. For example, one may enter indigenous populations or hubs that offer informational contrast to their current reality. They may do so to the extent that the vitality of the prior center, the home base, becomes diluted. Still, this does not suffice to actualize that new locality, because there is no vitality remaining in the original source. Attempting to do so forfeits the development of what it means to belong to a real civilization. One may be capable of actualizing that realm, but in doing so, the psyche recalls the prior actualizations, which proved more effective.

Even as the vitality of the prior center diminishes, it will be highlighted if directly threatened by a mediocre actualization. Here, we must recognize that existing actualization must always be acknowledged for its stature, not merely its vitality, as it has been imprinted upon consciousness. Once a realm of consciousness is explored, it cannot revert to a prior state. For example, once one understands the notion of clothing the body at a conscious level, one cannot revert; even if they act otherwise, they merely occupy a notion that no longer aligns with their psyche's knowledge.

This is why former memories remain pertinent to a mature state of mind, even after their vitality has waned. The imprint remains significant so long as a more promising form of consciousness is being explored. Thus, an indigenous person who enters a geographical or political reality of higher stature, at least in terms of consciousness, is no longer bound by their former realm, except through the connecting framework required to retrieve its vitality. Subsequent actualizations will always be more prevalent and nourishing to conscious experience, replacing the former frame of reference, since it was inferior. Yet vitality remains a matter of negotiation, as the psyche requires recognition of its effects, even within new actualizations.

Dynamics of Context: Influence on the Psyche

Context is a formidable aspect. When used correctly, it becomes a healthy utility of the psyche; when used incorrectly, it can lead to its decline. When context is applied to an interactive locale (a context-dependent space that engages participants through internal rules and symbolic roles rather than direct consciousness) , or even more so to an embodied locale, such as one with a high degree of sociality, it can serve as the entrance to substantiate one's share or place in that location. There is a pedigree to this: whatever the locale is, it is not for its own sake but rather as a formation for a degree of study, much like the Amazon serves the scientific community for its research.

Alternatively, context can actualize that locale and disrupt the psyche. The difference between these two forms of context is the outside-in versus the inside-out method. When the context is that of a foreigner surveying a new location, it brings a conscious sentiment into that locale for extraction. When the context is only to stimulate the internal state of that locale, there is no extraction, for it is, in itself, the point of interaction. There is no extraction because one does not view the experience as external, but rather as a home in itself.

Therefore, context will actualize the locale by forming internal mechanisms, having the individual entrenched in the realization that they are related only to that locale and no other. For example, if one were to take a contextual outlook, even if the ideas were of an origin that is transcendent to that locale, such as canonical practice, it would still only actualize the locale itself, because the context is only being used to promote the nature of that system. Without even knowing it, one can animate the internal system against the source of the context. So we arrive at the idea that even if the liberator of any tradition were to show up, there would be a contest since the source of the context is no longer applicable. Rather, the realization of the locale itself becomes the purpose.

Of course, external information is needed because the locale is a desolate tract, after all, and does not have enough of its identifiable vitality to produce an expansive library that assembles at its fringes. However, the source of that material is being used to give credence to the internal system, instead of serving its original purpose: to be understood and applied in this makeshift locale.

The process is such: the sourced material is brought forth, but then it is contextually altered so that it appears to be an internal manifestation. Once there is social acceptance as a context sourced in itself, it will take on the form of actualizing the locale against the true nature of that source.

Of course, we do not seek the dismantling of these locales, for they are essential in their purpose, and are only beneficial when they appear to have some sort of authenticity and this can only happen when individuals take upon themselves the task of actualization. Yet, this should only occur from within; an expansion toward the outside. Once the individual is educated from the outside, they certainly cannot reenter into the internal project of stabilization.

For instance, if one is raised in an internal locale, even if there is noticeable stimulation and emanation from the outside, because that is not their core education, they are nearby to build and maintain the existing system. A resort town, or a seasonal locale such as a beach or park, runs most adequately when it is maintained by those who are internal and who have never substantially breached the outside. They are simply raised in that system so that their psyches can actualize without a detriment to themselves or others. Although they do not have access to a clear pathway of consciousness, they are developing a preliminary state of an interactive locale for the moment when they do arrive to the external realm.

Even if the context appears the same, meaning the same content, by the very virtue of perspective, one will extract, and the other will actualize. Thus, we see that context can be used to the detriment of the psyche if we consider its comprehensiveness, or to its benefit if we attend to its detail and understanding, seeing the whole as a good thing.

In this perspective, context is the bridge or the abridgement of a system. It is the bridge to connect to higher systems, or the abridgement to reallocate the thing itself with the thing itself. In this analogy, we can take it a step further: the abridgement will have the purview smaller than the prior state. For if one chooses to bridge something within itself, it must be viewed as more concise, not more elaborate.

The continued use of context in this way would lead the psyche to adopt a very distinct and repetitive perspective on itself, so that one merely stands on that notion and no other. Further prolongation would cause the psyche to consolidate to the point where no further extraction of expansive information is possible. One would then become a shadow of their former state, losing the ability to stand upon more than a single measure of consciousness.

When context is applied to a consciousness locale, or its parts in succession, it can either serve as a bridge, to the psyche's detriment, or as a temporary vantage point, to its benefit. Specifically, if one brings context, especially a strong form, into a consciousness locale, it should serve the source of that context, rather than overpowering or distorting the psyche's natural flow. This ensures that the context enhances the experience without subverting the core of the individual's consciousness.

Socialization of Political Information

The league of information received by the individual can either be laid by an existential ramification or a conceptual imprint. In the case of political information, it will always be conceptualized from the inception because it is based on a construct rather than on a material experience at the individual level. No single person experiences the state and its embodiment directly, but rather as its construct. Every format of information disseminated from anything related to political relevance is conceptually based.

What differs about information from a conceptual inception is that it is sensed as though it is part of a book format, so that it is not inherently connected to fundamental sociality or biological manifestation, and therefore can only be considered in terms of how one broaches the subject and contrasts with it, rather than being served as a subject itself. We recognize this at a fundamental level, for nobody would want any sphere of social experience to be completely politicized; for that necessarily carries a negative connotation, despite the prevalence of the necessity for political organizations.

Because political information is highly dramatized, people often treat it as existentially significant, even though, in reality, it is just content in an archive.

The transfer of such information also participates in that agenda, so that it can be socialized to imbue a sentimentality of being more than a context-based item. A political discourse can broach the subject, spreading it among individuals in a dynamic and existential fashion, to a point where it is not merely a political data stream emanating from its archive, but rather a socialized manifestation of its substance. It is the details extracted from its conceptual forerunner that pertain to private and socialized affairs.

This new form of information will differ in construct from the original political sentiment, depending on how much existential participation has been added to the stream of context. It is the same matter as with any archival extraction: although initially purely conceptual, the book stands in time as a mere inanimate object, not on par with anything existential. But as the reader extracts the data and socializes contained by their internal database, especially through external discourse, it becomes existentially relevant; it initiates the amending process of that procedure.

If we follow the final product of that socialized sentiment, it is embedded with existential demarcation, but still retains the original conceptual forerunner. The source of this sentiment was purely arbitrary, and we must recognize it as such if we are to consider it part of the infrastructure in developmental sociality. However, by the time we reach its later stages, the socialized particles of that final product have become the existential manifestations, pronounced through the lens of the original concept.

And in the manner that socialized development and existential demarcation partake in that conceptual originality, and in placating the arbitrariness of the original conceptual source contrasted with the later existential development, one finally has a product that is genuinely real and part of infrastructure.

Now we can easily develop the complexity of that archival database of conceptual information, whether political, its subcategories, entertainment, or other formidable industries, so that it still remains a conceptual database up until the process of extraction occurs. Until someone suggests that the subject itself is arbitrary, merely a database for extraction that never becomes more than that, it will continue to be regarded as a source of existential significance. In reality, it only serves the agenda of extraction toward a presumed existential relevance, but has none of its own.

The social transmission appears to engage in an existential exercise, presented as though it were an inherent biological imprint. In reality, it is nothing more than another form of a conceptual process. One is not engaging dynamically with those mediums of communication, but rather is still considered part of the archival requiring further extraction. Although the sense data may be traumatized, it remains bound to the realm of the conceptual database, much like an illustrated book remains bound to its textual content. The additional imagery in the book does not add a deeper existential layer, just as extra sensory data does not provide more existential depth to a conceptual process. An illustrated book, for instance, may appear richer, but it still follows the same basic data processes as a plain document, which can lose its effectiveness when it struggles to describe a conceptual idea.

Although a picture may seem to exist beyond the realm of conceptuality, much like a computer database, it merely follows the same data input processes as any other form of computation. In the case of the illustration, it operates under the same concept, despite prevailing perceptions that it possesses greater existential depth.

It does not help that it is used as evidence of an existential reality, making picture and film highly significant elements in contemporary justice, all because they appear to involve an existential player more dramatic than a simple conceptual layout. However, if we follow the psyche and examine its nuances in addition to its acceptance of a picture as a framework of reality, we see that it is not received as an existential experience but rather as a highly volatile conceptual process.

Photographers will note this, and in fact, the industry of photography is its greatest evidence, that it is the creation of the picture more so than the existential reality of the picture. There would be no need for the creation and complexity required of the trade of photography if it were to create the existential reality as it was, for then simply the picture itself would suffice, and any tinkering with that process would delineate and disestablish that objective.

The subject itself, such as the evidentiary picture, responds to the perception of the psyche as a format of intellectuality that cannot be experienced when one sees the infrastructure to which the picture is based. The photographer, when attempting to take a mental image of a scenario, would be attempting to conceptualize and apply a framework to that very existential data, like any art form.

Interaction of Contextual Domains

Before we can explore how contextual layers operate interactively, we must consider how context breaks down under pressure. Through the contextual overlay or the interactive component, one will not find absolute personhood accessible. Contextual exploration seeks to clarify what aspects of personhood remain accessible or ambiguous when filtered through varying social and psychological frameworks. The same can be said for the interactive component: if a single limb or aspect becomes sensible, the rest will be set aside for later reference.

Regardless of the contextual interest, we can identify an interactive component that allows it to manifest, even if only as a distant relationship. We might like to say that the wholeness of consciousness is behind the interest of contextual exploration, but we must assume the contrary. While it can be said that such wholeness is possible, for personhood should lead toward its manifestation, more likely, a component of personhood becomes the driving force.

In some sense, context serves as the disambiguation of the psyche and body, allowing personhood to reside at a specific referential point. It approaches the subject of its mental interest with a vitality that should be allotted alone. In this way, contextual information can be followed without the regular wavelengths of dependency. The problem of personhood is that it is part of the environment and social reality, which become resistant to purposeful and transparent exploration, exploration that is deserving in the absence of environmental and social overlays.

Therefore, a disruption of reality is needed to form a bubble of a new domain, one which can develop its details before returning to home base. For instance, the contextual domain of education is always structured to be apart from the environment. We might say that education cannot occur while simultaneously attached to the social reality that lies beyond its front doors. This separation allows for a curriculum of study to be enhanced and received, irrespective of its parallels with sociability.

A common theme emerges: "What does this material assist with in the reality outside of it?" To this, one should reply, "Exploration cannot be absolute if it parallels reality." Contextual material manifests against the movements of reality. The choice of contextual information for study revolves around general themes which share a common thread. It cannot be information immediately germane to reality, as that would imply a function of providing contextual guidance within the social sphere. What results is the inability to recognize the social reality; who can follow with such precision?—and an inability to interact with the contextual material, as it contradicts social norms.

Thus, a governing theme arises in education: the material must be unrelated to the current social reality but embody universal themes that can predictably interact with social reality in the decades to come. We must envision the future, providing themes that will appropriately parallel it. If the focus is too deliberate, one will begin to include social reality as they imagine from the present moment. Firstly, they contain only their unique perspective. Secondly, yesterday's social reality differs from today's. Thirdly, the contextual material must remain available for future use, as the moment of readiness for interaction may coincide with a social reality that has already passed. Fourthly, by offering themes relevant only to the present, there is no provision for later adaptability. This is why universal themes are ideal, they are always present, hovering, ready to be adapted to an evolving social reality.

There are many universal themes which have not become institutionalized. For instance, certain identities maintain universal themes that are not regularly developed within a Western tradition. This is why universal themes must be transmittable into the traditional stronghold, which is institutionalized for the coming age.

When universal themes are taught contrary to institutionalized segments, they are lost to oblivion, irrelevant points of interaction in the ongoing social conversation. They may emerge momentarily, and as such, we can theoretically assume legitimacy for any theme. However, the future often reveals itself as a continuation of the already institutionalized themes. Even if a new universal theme is introduced, it takes much deliberation and exhaustive eras before it becomes properly etched into systematic thinking.

In example, certain art forms have been included into the institutionalized canon due to its continuous deliberation through centuries. There are many art forms that have not yet been institutionalized, yet are worthy of inclusion in higher education due to their adaptability to various aspects of life. However, they often remain in the background until they are eventually formalized within an institution. Once the universal theme is institutionalized it becomes a habitat for continuous interaction through the supposed life of any developing citizen. Thus, education would be the supposed life to be lived according to institutionalized universal themes that will readily interact according to social reality. Anything external to those parameters would be individualized education that proposes a personal addendum that leaves one to reattach the material to the social conversation.

The weakness of universal themes lies in their connection to the details of practical reality. For instance, a universal theme might be medical analysis, or more precisely, the study of an organism and the synchronization of its parts to create a sense of wholeness. This is as universal as we can become within the medical field. We could say it's an exploration of nature, though this mislays specificity.

Once we accept it as is, we may lose accuracy, specifically in the medical field. Once this is established, we can understand that anything undergoing analysis that provides details of the synchronization of parts of organisms will be of interest for this contextual material. If we understand that a flesh wound needs to be tended to in order to stop the flow of blood, we can translate that to its universal theme.

The organism depends on its blood circulation to distribute it, and without a sufficient resupply, it would be detrimental to the organism's wholeness. From this universal theme, we would not immediately identify that external blood loss can be problematic for the organism, as it is the details of practical understanding that provide this insight. What informs us that excessive blood loss is detrimental is the organism's dependence on blood. The individual's attachment to their own selfhood makes them a recognizable agent within the organism's dependencies.

When the organism perceives the loss of that dependency, it recognizes its state of decline. This is coupled with traditions, based on material experience, that losing blood equals a harmful state for the organism. Therefore, the reason an individual intuitively knows that blood loss is problematic is through traditional experience and an awareness that blood supply is crucial for the organism. If the organism is remote from being exposed to other organisms, we might wonder whether it would learn to recognize its dependency on blood circulation. It is, however, through traditional contexts that most organisms learn such dependencies from an early age. An individual applies this traditional knowledge of an organism's dependencies to their subjective experience of blood loss.

This process is evident throughout medical material of any level of sophistication. There is contextual material that is an insulated study, separate from individuation and adaptability. Since an individual is subjectively placed within their own organism, it is usually the case that any medical context would be adaptable to the organism. One can safely assume that wherever their medical exploration leads them, it will be adaptable to the organic structure.

However, this is only the specific vantage point of the organism in its propagation of life. This perspective doesn't address other aspects of life but focuses solely on the propagation of the organism and its organic continuation. We could argue that the organism can propagate despite its organic decline, just as a wise, aging individual may offer remedies of extreme importance.

Thus, we identify the weakness of contextual material as being adaptable only to a very specific theme within the continuum of wholeness. However, we could also expand on what has been said. We could understand blood loss, as a liquid, to be a dependency and notice how we are drawn to liquids over solids. We could then understand a social context in which people value smooth or fluid interactions. We can also interpret the color red as both a dependency and a representation of vitality, so that whenever we encounter red, we appreciate its dual significance.

The reason we want to universalize contextual material is that it allows us to attach other contextual information and its coinciding subjective experiences. If we follow a medical term with a very specific focus, we will not be able to connect much else to it. For instance, we might attach it to a traditional medical history, thus linking it to history itself, but beyond that, it's difficult to connect further. If we universalize the contextual material to a higher degree of appropriateness, we can cross-examine it with other contexts.

When the process becomes too universal, if we attribute any medical element to be part of a universal system deserving of a dynamic approach across all known systems, we won't have much to work with in terms of contextual application. Not every specific interest warrants a universal order. For example, a broken limb can be recognized within the framework of all other limbs because limbs function within a widespread system. However, the distinct limb deserves unique attention that does not fully network with all other limbs. Yet, we could universalize the specific limb to apply contextual overlays in reference to that peculiar limb in its various contexts.

This highlights that not every universal system is worthwhile for attention, but rather, only those aspects that are adaptable. If we perceive the limb as singular among a system of limbs, we lose the ability to adapt to other contexts. We cannot focus solely on a system of limbs in addition to its application to other contextual material due to the deficiency of attention that the experience demands. Indeed, the broken limb will continuously stimulate the psyche, guiding further exploration.

When universalized in this manner, we disrupt the system by differentiating it, and we quickly reach the limit of adjacent adaptability. Another important point is that the universalization of any material must not differentiate but rather appropriate its unique expansion. If we perceive a human being's decline as part of nature's natural decline, we disrupt the exposition. We differentiate the human being from nature's decline, and as a result, there is no stimulus for exploration. We could say that degeneration in nature aligns with its synchronization, and components of nature depend on a system that is self-conscious of its own faults. However, there is no stimulus for exploration because the concentration is on the human being and its decline.

For a more practical example, if we determine that a certain food causes "x," we can universalize this by asserting that foods, in general, cause multiple determinants. However, we cannot connect an adjacent context that will remain tied to the specific food. We could say that the organism is a chemical system in which everything has a determinant. This can, for instance, provide subjective appropriation in social systems, where everything has a determinant, whether from speech or activity. However, in doing this, we lose connection to the original stimulus, how a particular food causes "x." What happens is that we've differentiated from the specificity of that particular food for the sake of universality.

Now, let's approach the example without differentiation: Certain food causes "x." To universalize this, we can follow the specificity of the stimulus. This specific food also reminds us of a certain personality or character. Thus, the stimulus provides a contextual overlay about personalities that parallel the determinants of the food, e.g., animal consumption causes energy, which aligns with an active-oriented lifestyle. We cannot universalize this further without losing the original stimulus, but we can broaden it to other contextual overlays.

It is understandable for an individual to incessantly universalize up the point of including the wholeness of personhood or reality. Because specificity cannot be universalized without losing its attachments, we can only choose factual universality, despite the loss of particulars. The most that becomes possible is to broaden specificity to many lateral contextual overlays. The same can be said for universality which applies most effectively to particulars.

The reason medical contextual layers are a potent reference point is that they are always adaptable to the organism which studies them. The one caveat of the medical contextual layer is that it may lack a universal structure applicable across all spectrums. The success of this material is that it addresses a very specific aspect of the organism. To universalize that aspect would be to perceive a dynamic system that would differentiate from the material at hand, and we would lose the original focus. What's necessary, then, is a broad approach to the specifics, allowing them to remain adaptable in their own sense. When specificity is too diluted, it's highly improbable to apply or adapt it to any other contextual field. It adopts a new language, minuscule details, and embellishments that limit its nuance and adaptability. However, if we take a dynamic approach and perceive a universal system within the organic structure, those particulars will be lost, and success will be mitigated.

Both contextual layers, a more universal perspective and a detailed analysis of particulars, are necessary for success. What can't offset with microscopic analysis can be distributed through a universal practice of organic systems. There's no right or wrong in this analysis because nature paradoxically deals with both general and specific. Each can lead to the other by suggesting directions for navigation.

If certain particulars highlight material, we can approach the universal system with interest in those nuances to further an overall theory. For example, terminology can identify a historical lineage, from classical antiquity to the present era. This is a universal approach to fairly specific material that is utilized. When in communion with these particulars in current practice, there is no space for historical lessons, only for the material it provides in respect to progress. That bubble represents the microscopic necessity to focus on the subtle particulars of the organic system. There's no great entrance from social reality into these confined domains because that would attempt to fix the paradox of nature. Instead, within these limited domains, one applies as if it is the only realm of occurrence. When the stretch concludes, the individual returns to the universal order, reflecting on what has been learned.

At a later interval, those subtle learning experiences will form an applicable framework for universal themes. This is much like how gravity was once a theory of domain-specific details and has become an equation for the center of selfhood, in how there is a concept of the "gravity" of experience or situation. Centering selfhood will always be understood through the theory of gravity, which represents the universal manifestation of detailed, domain-specific analysis.

Whatever develops within the setting of social reality will not be pure contextual exploration but rather a universal process of integration. This is why an identity will struggle in conversations within the universal social order. The demand upon the body is such that one must align with the current conversational theme, while contextual developments do remain static. For the return of conceptual developments to the wholeness of personhood, or more accurately, the environment and social reality, it must assert its own merit. The two cannot coincide because we depend on the wholeness of anything, personal or social.

Yet, we must consider where the contextual material rests when it seems to be lost to a greater order; it naturally arises later in the conversation, in greater detail. Not all contextual information will be settled, but only that which can enhance the ongoing conversation. The truth of the matter is that initially, the incentive for contextual interest aligns with social reality. Theoretically, one can explore anything within a bubble, but contextual interest naturally aligns with that wholeness. An aspect of personhood represents the wholeness because, in its segregation, it expands to become a counterpart.

There is, however, the case of an individual deviating from the wholeness of personhood by following a very specific contextual interest that doesn't interact with present social reality. The outcome is that, once integrated into the totality of reality, the material proves inapplicable and ends up as an unused database. It may, however, gain relevance if and when social conditions shift closer to a point of contextual alignment.

The traumatic instance is an interactive moment that incorporates a significant portion of personhood, and thus, will underline the contextual manifestation for an extended period. The underlying nature does not dictate detailed interest but a general direction based on conclusive suppositions of the event. When one wants to engage more deeply with the event, they can interact with its sensory and intricate details. This allows further manifestation, resulting in a more nuanced direction, rather than a general one. Just as a poetic moment may either simplify complex dimensions or introduce complexity in place of an inaccessible comprehension of its layered content, it remains equally open to interpretation in both ways.

Context and Codependency

There is a relationship between context and codependency, and it is timely to highlight it. The more contextual layers embedded in an interaction or relational object, the greater the potential for high levels of intimacy. Context is a gate, but it is also the creation of a structure that necessitates a gate and consequently contains substance within it. Without context, without the gate, there is no structure, and therefore the domain within the structure becomes inaccessible.

Thus, we must create a gate which compels a structure to be envisioned, allowing a domain of substance within its confines to be interacted in an intimate manner. One might suggest that the process should be reversed, that we first build a structure and then provide a gate to enter. However, if we study a structure closely, we find that its quintessential point lies in its ability to contain a residing element.

The gate is not only an entrance from externality to internality but is also the first point from which the rest of the structure can be built. We could imagine a demolished house with only its doorway intact it would still appear as a kind of domain. By contrast, a structure fully enclosed without a gate appears merely as a sealed box, denying any sense of internality and rendering it passive within the geographical plane. The gate begins the conversation of what constitutes internality versus externality, thus, context is the foremost recipient of intimacy.

As mentioned, the more elaborate the layers of context, the higher the degree of intimacy; akin to the innermost chamber of any structure being its most intimate locality. Yet this model comes with a caveat: a contextual gate between each room, leading toward the innermost components, must be capable of both receiving externality and providing internality at each interval.

We recognize the innermost room of any structure by recognizing the level of importance of each room, following a chain of reactions until we arrive at the most important room, which evolves from this chain of potency.

Each room, and by that, we mean each gate, provides a certain provision to the entirety of the structure in its internality contrasting externality. For example, the living room is an important room whereas leading to the bedroom is even more important. If the kitchen led directly to the bedroom, we might question the possible intimacy of the bedroom, since the kitchen is less paramount than the dining room, and still has led to the bedroom.

Another point: the bathroom within the bedroom is not more intimate than the bedroom since it does not contain a context that could contend with the bedroom and therefore results as an externality of the bedroom. It is perceived that the bathroom is an additional layer, not the core space of interaction of the layout.

We can identify two aspects that allow context to transition smoothly between its layers: [1] the preceding context that has led to this context, [2] and its ability to be a more potent context than the proceeding layer.

For example, consider a married person who is engaged in an interaction with a single person of sexual possibility. The measure of context needed to demonstrate that this subsequent intimacy does not contend with the marital formation of intimacy is quite intricate. It is easy for such an interaction to become the innovative core space of interaction, while layering the marriage interactions as merely additional to it.

We are stating that context not only fosters intimacy but also protects interactions by preventing the natural inclination toward higher contexts that lead to greater intimacy. In this instance, the natural context would be one of deep intimacy due to sexual interest, as biological procreation and its subsidiaries are quite persuasive. One immediately enters into an engagement that claims the core space of interaction at the outset, without doing anything.

Therefore, more rooms, meaning more gateways, are necessary to lead from marital intimacy toward this interaction. This helps alleviate the natural context that seeks to arise. Each gate wedged between the marriage-intimacy and the new interaction provides a lens to scope the scenario and ward off the commanding biological context.

For instance, a proper context for this kind of interaction might be an once-in-a-lifetime crisis experienced by the person of interest. The context of being empathetic in dealing with such a crisis inserts multiple wedges between the innermost chamber and this interaction. Instead of acting from a biological vantage point of sexual intimacy, the relationship is grounded in the empathetic assistance of distress. When the moment the crisis subsides, the context subsides with it, giving way to the preceding layer of biological intimacy. In this scenario, context does not serve to elevate intimacy, but rather refocuses one's energy toward a specific and particular aspect of intimacy.

We can now discuss natural context, which arises without any deliberate effort to build layers. In any interaction, whether of a sexual nature or not, natural context will emerge when there is no replacement in order. When two people interact without deliberate context, each will naturally enmesh with the other, as there is a biological context to fuse organisms together. This is the natural supposition of nature: it will revert to its laws, in which connecting organisms become one.

This is where codependency emerges. It is the result of normal contextual suppositions arising when there is no human interface to project a contextual layer of a different stature. In some sense, it is the most intimate because it is the most natural and incorporates the universality of personhood. A person becomes fused with another and can no longer find the space that distinguishes them.

Now we approach the subject of context that removes intimacy. When the contextual layer is so robust, as in the case of a house believed to be not only an internality save for existence itself in which the world is immaterial, it begins to lose its intimate layer. The working context in such a situation creates a space so intense that it prevents external interaction. Because of this, only a small aspect of selfhood can be entertained for intimacy. All external interactions, and their relevant components of personhood, are denied free exchange. Thus, context, while typically a protective measure that fosters intimacy, can become so robust that it inadvertently stifles further intimacy.

We can understand this by the earlier example where, as previously claimed, the bedroom is the innermost chamber containing the highest degree of context in a given structure. If the bedroom becomes the sole place of interaction and dominates the resident's day, it will lose its intimate orientation. This is because the rest of the structure is not allowed dynamic interaction by means of the bedroom and thus prohibits the flow of context between each room and the outside world.

Conversely, if the bedroom is enclosed most of the day and not utilized dynamically, it will not receive the context it deserves. Consider this: if all doors within the structure are opened and closed by social participants, the entire structure becomes capable of receiving contextual exposition and experiencing intimacy relative to each room, including the doorway to the external world. However, if that external doorway is not used in a similar fashion, the structure cannot receive external contextual exposition, and internal exposition comes to a halt. However, if the doorway is always open and always used, the structure loses its sense of internality and becomes a public space in terms of intimacy and context.

When the homebody is external the structure, we can evaluate their public interactions to determine whether they are beneficial or problematic for the home structure. If they interact in a manner that treats the household doorway as open for exposition and closed for digestion, it will prove beneficial. If the interactions are to be considered irrespective of the household doorway and in effect to assume that the door is shut and the interaction is a comprehensive reality unto itself; the structure ceases to be a habitat of privacy and intimacy.

For example, in the situation above, where one meets a single person of sexual interest and engages with intimate sensibility, the doorway for information exposition within the household will immediately be assumed to extend to an additional locality, corresponding to the new intimate setting, much like how a bathroom is connected to a bedroom. The household is not lost for all intimacy but only becomes a subsidiary to the newfound intimacy. This of course depends on the measure of contextual layers that are wedged within that interaction which may prove to be adequate to allow this intimate interaction to be an additional room of the prior household instead of the reverse.

The idea is this: as long as the interaction on the external front is universal, it can incorporate the private life into its intimate structure. The challenge of engaging with sexual connotation stems from its lack of universal grounding. Were it otherwise, the preexisting intimacy associated with the homebody would be carried into the interaction, constraining the emergence of a separate, individualized form of intimacy.

By contrast, intimacy with the universal spectrum, general concepts, major cities, communal entities, the supernatural, can integrate all, allowing for the universal incorporation of the parts of personhood, including the homebody and its intimate layers. This of course depends if the cities, communal settings, divine interests, are interacted in its universal form. Although if one interacts intimately with a communal entity that does not reveal its universal framework, it will renounce certain aspects of personhood in this intimate function. This is how the global enterprise is acknowledged and respected by the community.

Of the three, communal entities are most prone to problematic interaction, as they are not permanently situated within a universal hierarchy. For instance, common bureaucratic institutions or general academia, both quite embedded in the universal system, would not be a recipe for private intimacy. That being the case, it is specifically these two institutions that lack the most intimacy, since they are universal by constitution and do not offer a sense of locality for intimacy to emerge.

Still, they can be interacted to provide provisions of intimacy on condition the individual places contextual wedges that foresee aspects of locality within that universal picture. Those segments of locality which result in intimacy are embedded in the universal picture and therefore do not negate prior intimacy. The problematic nature of the third aspect mentioned, supernatural interaction, is that it depends on one's understanding of the supernatural, which either places the interaction in a universal setting or as a locality that does not encompass the whole array of personhood.

Another problematic aspect, which is apportioned within universal systems, is that one can overly interact with the universal setting and thus become codependent and devoid of personhood. When this happens, all prior intimacy halts because the dominant contextual layer overpowers the rest. Its information relay absorbs the individual into the object of interaction. Even though this is a universal system and is characteristically opposite to personhood, it nevertheless renounces personhood in respect to universality to become overly intimate with that structure.

Necessity of Contextual Externalities

The area of growth within a certain domain parameter is limited by a certain evolution of its internality. The only manner to approach a nuanced perspective of a domain is through a novel domain that serves to reflect back upon its setting. The new domain is a contextual service and nothing more, for it does not take the space of an existential reality, that is the situation in the area upon which this purposeful reflection is based. While there may be a biological experience, such as relying on this locale and partaking in all the necessities of the organism, the entire enterprise is a research project. This is the notion of travel, exile, or vocation, where the new locale is a service to the existential one.

The juncture at which the external locale is most necessary is when the existential participation is so engendered to where it ingests its perpetual state in place. The notion that something ingests itself is the experience of an existential participation that has exceeded its limit, which, instead of providing the habit of a center, begins to act as the center that precludes individual participation.

For this reason, when the point of existential participation has reached the ingesting point, the solution is for an innovative locale to provide a reflection point. Many cases reach a point of existential ingestion (a state in which an individual is fully consumed by their current role or reality, losing reflective distance) that has removed such individuation whereas the innovative locale takes up precedence as a new existential center. This is rather a misappropriation of the sequence, which presumes the novel locale as an existential territory all the while serving as a reflection of that exhausted existential center.

We can hypothesize that existential exhaustion arises from two distinct factors: one, from a divergent direction that reaches its maximum capacity without relegating the interventions of other elements of the psyche; and the second, from the psyche itself, which has participated from all of its major vantage points until the juncture was met with exhaustion. We can term the latter as realistic exhaustion. Every juncture that has a single direction and becomes exhausted from existential participation could be presumed to include the exhaustion of the entire psyche. Only upon a conceptual detachment of the existential participation does one acknowledge that there exists a major variety of approaches to further stimulate the attachment. When the juncture arrives where there is no simulation to take effect for the existential attachment, it becomes realistically exhausted.

In this context, there is a need for an innovative and tangible space, both physical and conceptual, that invites participation and reflection. This space serves as a new gateway for engagement, standing in contrast to the divide between abstract existential detachment and concrete material transformation designed at forming a unique existential connection. When a domain is interpreted through a singular psyche framework, existential detachment alone may suffice to generate an alteration in perspective and bring renewed intuition of the existential landscape.

However, detachment alone does not provide a portal to a comprehensive database of reflection; rather, it produces a landscape akin to a desolate tract, one that appears reflective but is, more accurately, an openness of exchange where the psyche can adopt new parameters.

This is why a reflection point of a novel locale can sustain the conscious exposition necessary for genuine reflection and remodeling, whereas the desolate tract only redirects preexisting information of the psyche. In other words, the desolate tract must remain interactive alongside the psyche, while the reflective locale can supply some of the provisions that the existential center once provided.

One does not simply "move on" from an existential center; either one conceptually detaches for an intermission, or reflects in a novel locale. The contextual domain serves the novel locale by providing the database of information that reflects back on the existential order. Once reflection reaches its maximum capacity, it may be misappropriated by the existential center, or have one return to the center for reintegration into existential reality. In this way, the cycle completes itself: the conceptual domain accumulates reflective data points, which are then inevitably brought back to the existential center as a new frame of reference.

After a period of engagement with the existential center, during which it reaches its ingestion juncture, the individual must seek out either a desolate tract or a truly novel conceptual domain. If the new domain remains too similar, its novelty limited, it will function merely as a bridge back to existential reality, rather than as a true point of reflection. Of course, there is also a necessary interval within the existential center for conceptual and material disengagement, ensuring that the psyche's entirety has been processed through rumination. Not all novelty qualifies as a contextual domain; for some, novelty itself constitutes an existential structure.

Prolonging Contextual Vitality

The researcher goes on an excursion to indigenous lands, lacking the civilized structure of their habitat, and utilizes a connecting framework from their conscious origins so that they never have to settle in that land in a way that actualizes themselves and makes them develop to be an indigenous character. It is quite an anomaly that a researcher can perform such a task for prolonged periods, or the soldier on a campaign, which can be years long, while maintaining an origin context that restricts and withholds resettlement and actualization in these domains. This illustrates how persistent internal context can shield individuals from fully engaging in new environments, both limiting and preserving intimacy.

The context of the researcher is based on the research map, so that their sole objective is to further their research. When the research becomes limited, hits a bottleneck, or reaches a culmination, they retract their foreboding steps. Of course, the vitality of that research context depends on the grandiosity with which the origin consciousness was engaged. A first-time researcher, for instance, will not be able to sustain too long a period, as their consciousness may not yet be deserving or capable.

Upon returning from the trip, the individual now has the momentum to reapply the context to the consciousness continuum. As time progresses, the reaffirmation of those consciousness sentiments gains further prowess. The intimacy and depth of the consciousness, including all the contextual gains from the research, contribute to a more stalwart position in that consciousness; as it so pertains to this context. The next research project will be infused with more consciousness sentiment for every exposition and extraction within that indigenous population. At each interval where research vitality diminishes, one can simply extract from the consciousness experience until they are resupplied for the contextual endeavor. With greater vitality from the origins, the output also becomes more highly contextual, more directed and dynamic than before.

In this way, the promise of longer spans of continuance with the same contextual output may be shortened by the depth of each moment. If one seeks to extend a project considerably, they may retract a controlled amount, holding back from the full depth of vitality and instead tempering the potential facing them. Often, we find researchers pulling back from their full ability and capability, aware that the context will lose its vitality with each shallower conjecture, thus shortening the overall excursion. It may be possible to fulfill that vitality in a matter of weeks, yet the process is stretched into months, giving the impression of pursuing finer details, when in truth it may be a subjective effort to prolong their research period.

From an objective standpoint, a detailed research analysis receives more attention and reception. However, this is not necessarily the researcher's subjective output, only the consequence of aiming to fulfill an objective requirement. In terms of the researcher's vitality, it can be quickly exhausted, and fulfill the project only according to their potentiality, despite the objective reception of that process.

This is why we find overly intricate details that are deviations from the general theme of research, where anthropologists formulate complex linguistic understandings despite the primary aim of their research being to gain a greater understanding of primitive culture and its development.[i] The usual retort is that through linguistic understanding, we gain that prerogative. Yet, if we follow the subjective process, the field offers these deviations to prolong the vitality of their research, almost like rest days for workdays.

The same can be said for a military campaign, in which the only objective is to succeed in military aims respective of their country of origin, specifically because that is the entire objective of the campaign. However, we find that there are many resolutions that do not require the resources of a certain campaign and instead are followed because they prolong the period of the campaign. Even the word suggests this, for instead of being a resolution between states, it is considered a campaign, taking on a further complex system of objectives that deviate from the genuine objective.

Through the lens of history, we can acknowledge the futility of certain warfare, which can only be surmised as a willingness to prolong the period of that campaign, irrespective of the vitality and consciousness with which the campaign had as its origins. "Continuance exists only for its own sake. It progresses with increasingly diluted logic, held together only by a faint contextual thread linking it to its origin, but not developed enough to extract and exhaust that vitality.

In this limbo, we have an illogicality that remains a sort of logical process, utilizing just enough to continue, but short of ever finding the exhaustive state. The researcher finds themselves in this predicament, where they acknowledge that, at the expense of fulfilling the vitality in true course, the directive of their entire endeavor will be depleted, as well, the objective perception of their accomplishments diminished.

With these two principles as their focus, they will extend as much to fulfill the objective perception of the research, with little subjective vitality getting in the way, and to continue the directive of the endeavor for the sake of directive alone; as if by reverting course they are unfulfilling a past directive. The same is true for the military campaign, in which they have at their disposal the ability to fulfill the vitality of their origin directive in a complex usage of their potential, or to continue to prolong the campaign for two principles. First, to perform the continuance of the directive for the sake of the directive, to not appear that they must leave the confines of their first directive, as it would retract upon their consciousness, affirming that it was all futile. And secondly, they will endeavor the prolongation in order to fulfill an objective point of success, despite the subjective vitality which will be stretched for the process.

This objective perspective of success is not the entire picture of the situation, but only what would be perceived as war aims, and not statehood necessities. The state has only the need for protection and resolution, and the objective perception of the endeavor is only the façade according to a specific narrative; it is usually the case that objective aims come at the cost of subjective vitality. Thus, we find states that will degenerate in order to fulfill the objective aim, which cannot be a subjective viewpoint.

As well, with the researcher, often the objective accomplishment may be at the cost of subjective aims, in which one must either avoid the added material that deviates from the theory or indulge at the expense of the core themes, usually the core themes are rejected.

It is possible for the researcher, especially the anthropologist, who begins to settle among the indigenous population, to do so for the mere fact that their research begins to intrude upon material that requires empathetic modality. So that when they return to their origin destination, they become part indigenous and part civilized. Researchers working in fields unrelated to direct cultural engagement will not have the same impact, as their work does not require the empathetic understanding involved in navigating the complexities of the regions in which they reside.[ii]

We will not find the same parallel in the campaign, because the soldier's entire composition is based on the military objective of the country of origin. The moment they begin to settle in those locales, it goes against the military objective and they lose the stature of being a soldier.

Now, let's revisit a point we discussed regarding representation. The soldier, in the course of their research or campaign, must engage interactively with the surrounding context. Since context involves the arrangement and regulation of the entire psyche's content, a specific mode of interactivity is necessary to process and navigate the information, despite the overwhelming nature of that context.

Therefore, the soldier, outside of strict campaigning endeavors, must participate in the rest of the psyche and engage in forms of interactivity, commodities, and amenities that do not pertain directly to campaigning affairs. Without this requisite, the soldier becomes dampened and lost to the context itself, unable to disseminate the campaign's context and interactive space. Consequently, they lose their composure and attachment to the context, since the dissemination of that material is not foreboding; instead, the context becomes directive with no personal basis. The rest of the psyche's propagation becomes a mere skeletal version of contextual attachment, and thus the campaigning endeavor loses its vitality, retaining only its strictest sense.

There we have it, that a lack of interactivity creates disorientation and dissociation from the context itself. Similarly, a researcher who fails to engage with the contents of the psyche, despite conducting research, will eventually lose their connection to the subject. This is why the anthropologist, through a high level of interactivity (albeit at the expense of actualizing in primitive territories), shows the most successful retention of attachment to the context of their research.

However, engaging with interactivity without foregoing context requires the dissemination of specific details and materials of that context, strictly within those parameters. While the anthropologist begins their interactivity by participating in the cultures they study, thus risking full actualization in those domains, the soldier would set campaign-contextual elements as a criteria for their interactive experiences.

Directing an element between the origin of consciousness and its dissemination in a contextual footprint will incur an overstimulation of material. Consider a developing writer's preliminary work: it is more guided by interactivity derived from consciousness but is overly obtuse, as if we meet their soul at the very first sentence. Comparable is a child's artistic journey, in which every element of their creation is a pronouncement of psyche happenstance originating in consciousness. In both cases, this directness is perceived as instruction in the relationship between writer (or artist) and reader (or reviewer), but in truth it is consciousness disseminating at a very high level.

This is why a preliminary writer cannot endure much time or circumstance in that expulsion of consciousness; it must be divulged in only a few instances. The same goes for preliminary artistic endeavors, which exhaust their expressive energy quickly. There is no separation between the origin of consciousness and the contextual endeavor; upon granting free will, it rapidly consumes its own vitality.

Indeed, a major area of research is preliminary artistic talent because it contains so much information within those origins of consciousness where later artistic endeavors lack. We are not simply studying childhood development but encountering an artistic landscape that offers insights into a high degree of consciousness, which becomes scattered and separated as development proceeds. The same applies to the preliminary writer: that fleeting expulsion of psychic contents and consciousness material allows research into its sub-layers.

However, unlike artistic research, studies of written forms typically focus on more complex works rather than the simplistic versions. Later research into artistic expression is not aimed at disseminating consciousness material but at understanding the objective form of art, irrespective of the artist. Similarly, research in written endeavors studies the author as an autobiographer, treating the content as autonomous sentiments to gain a deeper understanding of the art form.

Ultimately, all objective expression or art is potentially available for dissemination, but research gravitates toward the more profound forms because that is where society converges. We could take any text, gather socially, and expound its profundity to great depth, but in practice research focuses on works which have already gained prominence. These texts and artworks offer a stable ground in which most people can participate; lesser-known works lack that effect, not necessarily because they contain less depth or nuance.

If our assumption is correct, the most expressive expulsions of consciousness would provide the stand for profound research, since they contain unfettered and unmediated circumstantial content. Profound texts and art have already undergone a long process of complex relation between consciousness origin and contextual output, so the final product is a perfected form of objective development.

It is also more easily consumed because it lacks raw, blurting consciousness and is instead subdued in its hidden elements, elements that research then seeks to expand. Yet a simpler process exists in which one immediately gains entry to the consciousness of a preliminary, "infertile" text or artwork; the research can begin processing that consciousness from the outset. It is as if it's offered on a silver platter, leaving only the researcher to understand it. But researchers often decline this position, partly due to a lack of social convergence, these works lack objective development, and partly because researchers prefer to conduct complex contextual analysis that only brings consciousness to the fore at a much later stage.

Part 2: Intimacy

Foundations of Intimacy: Biology and Vulnerability

Having explored the architecture of context in shaping perception, we now turn to the second major theme: intimacy. This section investigates the biological, psychological, and social dynamics that allow for deep interpersonal and internal connection.

Intimacy is the experienced aspect of a conscious course that is received at the biological layer. This changes when the response is not paralleled with the degree of that exposition of consciousness, and so it becomes an external form of intimacy, reconstructed to fit the profile of the needs of conscious grounding, or more precisely, a prerequisite for grounding. An external form of intimacy is enough to satisfy the need for biological experience, as it doesn't take much to stimulate biological processes.

The location where an individual chooses to sleep often fosters an intimate association with both the physical space and its broader context.[iii] We would be wary of sleeping in a place that causes contextual synchronization contrary to our perspective of life, e.g., an enemy's domain, the relative of an intimate partner without their presence, or the dwelling of delinquents. Sleep is not presented in any manner other than biological necessity, consequently enduring an intimate experience from its manifestation without conscious deliberation. Already being the chosen activity, of which no other is possible or viable, entices the contextual material surrounding the setting keen on conscious and biological integration. However, in this instance, if someone believes they can sleep anywhere effortlessly (like a flight attendant), then sleeping in one place may feel less singular/intimate.

The contextual understanding arises through chosen activity, and this biological essential for sleep is not consistent in its relevance to its environment. Yet for such intimacy to take place, one must strip away a transcended contextual blueprint in order to be available for constant physical change. We could understand the vagabond to be overly preoccupied with their daily biological needs as they keep changing and are vulnerable to the present situation. While situational biological needs are predicted and not vulnerable to personhood, unless during major life transitions, the vagabond, being vulnerable to immediate needs, becomes consciously vacant to them. The reason a vacation grants a sense of intimacy is because biological vulnerability produces conscious grounding, which is usually absent during normal, predictable biological routines.

Biological vulnerability opens the system to recognize that this specific necessity is of extreme significance to every aspect of the psyche; much like when a person experiences a life-death scenario and becomes consciously available to the setting by means of all portions of the psyche. In the usual case of predictable biological activity, it does not stimulate the rest of the psyche due to its presumed and assumed nature. This changes when vulnerability allows every varying parts of the psyche to interact. For the rule of the moment is: the psyche is dependent on biological essentials as they necessarily become perceptible.

The vagabonds lose their sense of that vulnerability and instead accept biological activity in whatever comes their way. This is a case in point: whatever the biological experience becomes, if it's normalized, then it develops to be a concept in the conceptual realm. The normalization process removes the existential sense of biological dependency, even if a realized dependency remains. We cannot sustain constant awareness of every dependency or vulnerability in life. Instead, we are only asked to identify those outside of normalization.

For example, if one remains in an enclosed environment or contextual realm for an extended period, then the initial activities external to it will have a biological manifestation. Mere walking all the while experiencing of the environment will be recognized for its existential and biological nature. Thus, it will be endured as an intimate grounding, drawing the conceptual realm into the biological layer. Even when the biological activity is not a primary or major necessity, if it exists outside the realm of normalcy, it becomes intimate. This allows us to define intimacy as non-normative biological activity coupled with contextual excess.

Non-normative biological activity can be accessed through conscious deliberation instead of environmental dependency. This means that we can access any biological activity to find its existential experience, which runs throughout the psyche and creates intimate moments. Some aspects will naturally be compelled from the environment; like non-normative biological activity, conscious, or existential availability. This would mean that if the individual is consciously aware of their existential nature or the intricacies of their psyche, then whatever their environment, whether or not normative, becomes a habitat of intimacy.

The only way this can be avoided is through contextual succession, in which access is always dominant and not available for grounding due to continuous deliberation, having no availability for conclusively settlement.

The nature of contextual exploration is such that it will continue its logical format on the backbone of the biological aspects, finding no respite until it is removed from continuity; much like the research project, where the subject is thoroughly explored but does not become a repository of intimacy.

Similarly, the psychoanalyst may enter a degree of depth with strangers that even their intimate partner has no access, nonetheless without becoming intimate with them. To be wary of the one who does not expand their depth of study from all these encounters, as it is the case of inevitable intimacy which will disrupt the contractual relationship.

56

Conceptual Layer and Procreation

Intimacy is acquired by the fusion of biological continuity and conceptual layers. To be only conceptual and abstract, there would be no sense of personhood in that experience. While to be engrossed in biological continuity, either through sustenance or procreation, without a conceptual layer would result in a subjective sense that is not conceptualized. Intimacy occurs only when these two interact and create a haven of a conceptualized sense of self.

There is difficulty in approaching intimacy without a diverse array of proponents. This occurs because the aspects of the conceptual layer are only accessed through a biological demand for them. It wouldn't be enough for a single person to develop an expanded conceptual layer and re-enter their biological sense for the experience of intimacy. This is because the biological system has no inherent need for the conceptual layers, even as they are enjoyed. One entails conceptual layers according to biological continuity, and without that requisite, they hover above the biological sense unless conceptually integrated through dialogue.

The diverse proponents who engage in the biological sense will demand from each other the conceptual layers that fulfill what becomes missing through shared biological continuity. This demand is biologically engineered, and the conceptual layers will integrate in an absolute fusion that creates intimacy.

Immediately, we are struck with questions regarding the intimacy of procreation. If this theory is true, then it would require a diverse populace to experience a high degree of intimacy. If false, then the argument loses footing. Because only two people biologically create offspring, the conceptual aspects of intimacy must come from beyond personal biology. Therefore, we would conceptually generate a scenario of procreation that retains more diversity and, as such, more intimacy. Since biological continuity cannot be shared among many, the conceptual layers will not be biologically grounded.

Secondly, the sexual act is one that demands conceptual layers by its very nature. Since it concerns genetic continuity rather than personal continuity, it must be understood in terms of a concept of life, not just the socially agreed-upon notion of it. In contrast, sustenance, being about personal continuity, does not require a concept for the organism to sustain itself. Therefore, as long as conceptual layers are available, the sexual act will demand them for a fused formation of intimacy. Sustenance will not demand this unless involved in compromised food procurement, which introduces the need for conceptual layers.

We arrive at another distinction between personal continuity and lineage continuity: the degree of available intimacy. A single human is limited in both the number and diversity of their conceptual layers, which form their foundation; consequently, the degree of sexual intimacy they can achieve is limited. While an individual can explore conceptual layers with some success, their inherent biases prevent them from attaining true conceptual depth.

For instance, if one conceptually understands this discussion of intimacy, they may retain that layer with some degree of success. However, being bound to that understanding, they lack access to diverse opinions and perspectives. Even as one seeks personal diversity by attempting to understand other viewpoints, this cannot be done with ultimate success. If one remains in their private vantage point, they cannot fully engage with another; if they depart entirely, they merely adopt the other's perspective without integrating it. A multitude of vantage points cannot be fully experienced by a single individual, it becomes available only through a communion of dialogue.

A conceptual layer that does not engage in other vantage points lacks its distinctive depth. Every conceptual layer arises from an interplay of prior concepts. To believe that a single conceptual layer is the only valid perspective on reality is to overlook its inherent nature: it is always bound to, and in dialogue with, others. Such a view becomes overly simplistic, eventually stripping the layer of its connotation; much like a house detached from society ceases to be a home.

Dialogue, too, cannot produce depth unless it seeks to generate a vantage point that complements what the other lacks, while remaining accessible to the initiator. Yet even the most conceptually abundant dialogue does not grant access to the biological sense of experience, something only the organism itself can perceive. This is where communal nourishment becomes essential: it mediates conceptual intimacy through its process.

The concept of communal nourishment has no inherent limit on intimacy; it allows for diversity and the expansion of conceptual layering. This dynamic interaction can lead to profound intimacy. The usual limitation arises from the locality of communal nourishment, which often fails to engage its participants fully, especially in the absence of dialogue with highly conceptual individuals. When communal nourishment becomes merely an unpredictable display of ingestion materials, it requires no conceptual engagement. If it serves only one individual amid many, it becomes an act of dominion without expectation of retribution. Similarly, if the communal nourishment is bland or neutral , ignoring the unique biological and conceptual needs of each participant , it also imposes limits. Yet when these limits are lifted, intimacy can fill a vacuum of experience.

Intimacy through procreation is expansive: it includes even the slightest touch from another being. Facial or physical expressions associated with such touch become part of the intimate experience. The degree of intimacy is determined by proximity to the procreative moment; anything that alludes to such an instance carries heightened intimacy. Familial members who seek closeness also allude to procreation. Even among same-sex individuals, such interactions can evoke procreative associations, as biological continuity requires both selfhood and the opposite sex. A same-sex individual may represent closeness to selfhood, preparing for an encounter with the opposite sex. In pre-contact Hawai'i, sexual intimacy begins with same-sex encounters before transitioning to the opposite sex (Diamond, M., 2023).[iv]

Even in the absence of physical touch or explicit sexual acts, prolonged time together can awaken subconscious elements of procreation. These elements can enter dialogue, conceptually joining intimate associations. Dialogue itself can lead one into a conceptual realm where sexual associations emerge and deepen. When two people face each other, they inevitably reflect themselves through the other, initiating such associations.

The sexual realm begins with reflection on selfhood, which naturally leads to thoughts of biological continuity. When a system is reflected upon, its potential invites exploration. For example, assessing a structure's current state often reveals its future possibilities. We might thus claim, somewhat axiomatically, that reflection opens the door to potential. Yet intimacy cannot endure without conceptual layers, for their convergence creates the experience. While some interactions linked to sexuality may feel intimate, this is not always the case. Certain interactions may suggest sexuality yet lack any genuine intimacy. The experience depends on a conceptual layer, which is essential for both biological continuity and the intimacy that accompanies it.

When family members engage in physical touch, the conceptual layer varies depending on their history. If they have been apart, the layer reflects the dynamics shaped by that separation, often producing deeper love. Separation fosters conceptual engagement, intensifying the longing for reconnection. Sexual intimacy, in particular, relies on conceptual layers for fulfillment. As noted, it is unnecessary for the organism's development unless it involves reflection on selfhood and its potential for biological continuation.

Involuntary intimacy occurs when the conceptual layer is absent, yet an attempt is made to fabricate one. Even in feigned intimacy, a conceptual layer must form. By arranging the physical elements of intimacy, one hopes to justify the interaction conceptually. This is understandable, as it mirrors how communal nourishment , lacking direct biological impact , requires the activation of a conceptual layer. This approach may seem feasible for sexual intimacy, but it is flawed.

The error lies in misunderstanding the distinction: sexual intimacy forced into an occasion will indeed form a conceptual layer, but if that layer is used merely to compel a more complex one, the initial layer is excluded. Future occasions then depend on increasingly fragile layers until a proper conceptual foundation is found. The endpoint is a diminished drive for sexual intimacy, lacking even the seed of a conceptual layer to initiate the experience. Since sexuality depends on conceptual layers, when the foundation is weak, it resorts to whatever is available , often an impoverished version.

Sexual thoughts are always a fusion of conceptual and biological content. The conceptual aspect arises from the situation's potential: pleasure, experience, intimacy, human reflection, dynamic change, innocence and guilt (as expressions of potential and meta-dynamic change), involuntary or aggressive intimacy (as demands for conceptual layers), human vulnerability, and above all, biological knowledge. These are biological formations, as they seek either change in the current system or continuity in its future lineage. Traits are biological when they serve biological continuity: innocence signals openness to biological continuation, while guilt signals the same availability, but from the opposite end of the spectrum. A sexual thought is, by definition, a conceptual notion tied to biological continuity in the present system or its future lineage.

This reveals the power of sexuality: it neither allows a conceptual layer devoid of biological grounding nor a biological notion devoid of conceptual depth. It forms a near-perfect system, self-correcting by design. The limitation lies in its lack of diversity: it is bound to a singularity, preventing complex conceptual layers from fully participating in the occasion. This is why we avoid detailing specific examples of sexual thought content , because of its inherent simplicity. We cannot construct a complex version, as its singularity constrains it.

Communal nourishment, by contrast, offers vulnerability through unlimited conceptual depth. Its weakness lies in the complexity of the proper occasion , where intimacy becomes effective , and in its lack of biological singularity, which gives sexuality its experiential intensity. Attempts to merge the two, where each offsets the other's vulnerability, are fraught with difficulty. Such efforts lead communal nourishment into sexual activity, collapsing complex conceptual structures into singular, biologically driven experiences. The only way to expand sexual intimacy is through preparation: by diversifying one's mental aptitude through varied sexual and conceptual experiences. For instance, upon returning from the world, one integrates both the encountered sexual diversity and the conceptual abundance of those experiences, so that within the singularity of the sexual moment, the widest possible diversity is present.

The expansion of communal nourishment intimacy must not attempt to mimic the singularity and biological sense of sexuality, for doing so undermines the communal experience. Instead, intimacy is deepened by highlighting those aspects of communal nourishment that cultivate it. The vulnerability will always be there; compelling it past its natural limits risks collapsing the entire structure , much like a nonconformist communion. This is because communal nourishment intimacy, while more foundational to the system than sexuality, is less genuine in the experience of intimacy.

The rule is this: genuine intimacy will always replace a lesser form, even when the latter offers greater conceptual depth. When two forms of intimacy are equally genuine, the one with greater depth will prevail. When their depths are equal, the more genuine form dominates. Genuine intimacy is grounded in the sense that all participants share in biological continuity.

This conceptual framework , attempting to merge the sexual mainframe with its inherent limitations , will inevitably be discarded. Sexuality, being more genuine, will override any lesser form of intimacy. The result is a degraded version of sexuality, lacking conceptual depth. The conceptual richness fades as one approaches sexuality, while sexuality itself is diminished when used as a substitute for genuine conceptual complexity in a communal context. This form of sexuality will lack depth, failing to engage the singularity of biological continuity or lineage.

Though sexuality appears purely biological, it relies on a conceptual counterpart distinct from communal nourishment. Conversely, communal nourishment requires far less conceptualization for its experiential effect. One can lose appetite when all conceptual layers are removed ; communal nourishment relies on some conceptual engagement. Yet sexual appetite diminishes even more readily in the absence of conceptual layers. When focused intensely on a particular concern, one may be removed from the sexual realm, having lost access to the broader conceptual layers. Even then, they may still desire communal nourishment, albeit to a lesser degree.

Private Intimacy vs. Shared Consciousness

Let us take a moment to explore the interaction of a family body within such a nexus of consciousness. As noted, privatization creates intimacy pockets that do not partake in the wholeness of that consciousness. A private environment is natural for momentary experience, and in some sense, there is no access without a form of private perspective or ground.

As such, privatization endures a certain natural intimacy; however, it is always shadowed in comparison to that wholeness. Privatization cannot become a habitat for continuous use but must remain momentary to avoid exhaustion. The family body, likewise, must be understood as momentary in its experience. This balance is achieved when the family body engages in togetherness within that wholeness, rather than forming its own structure of privatization.

The point is this: the family body must be allotted only a portion of intimacy, proportionate to its environment and degree of privatization. Because both the environment and privatization are constantly changing, the family body is renewed in each interaction and is never static. The family body, in this context, refers to those who existentially exist alongside the continuous movement of the individual. This dynamic allows their presence contained by private moments to mirror that individual's inner movements accurately.

When this mirroring does not occur, due to various reasons, the family becomes like a private environment that produces intimacy in isolation. Whatever was gained exterior to the family body is then lost when intimacy occurs in such confinement.

Connection and Intimacy

To describe the difference between connection and intimacy, we must first identify each in their own regard. Connection is based on existential reflection, which is to say that it allows one the advantage of seeing themselves through the other. Intimacy, on the other hand, is existential experience, which, contrary to connection, is an engrossment of shared existence to a point of full integration. Although in another work we have stated that the integration is never complete, for the sake of contrast with connection, such a definition will suffice.

There is the notion that the mere experience of connection is a form of intimacy, as it involves a mode of sharing or exchange. However, since intimacy can arise even from the facial expression of a stranger, any discussion of it must refer to a measured quantity of intimacy. Intimacy does not necessarily require an exchange to occur. Simply touching another person can elicit intimacy. While a slight exchange may take place through the existential reflection of their own bodies prompted by the relevant touch of another, this is not the primary component of the experience. When discussing connection, it is the amount of exchange that qualifies it to be called a true connection.

Some may require a material exchange in moments of intimacy, and for good reason. Since intimacy entails existential integration, it involves a kind of merging of selves to allow for that integration. There is no defensive mechanism in place to prevent the post-integration process. As a result, one can be left simply abandoned or existentially lost. The exchange becomes handy so that all intimacy is checked by its exactness of exchange, thereby, even as one is risking being lost post-integration, they have equally exchanged beforehand, which would have them risk as much of a loss as they are to have gained. This will ensure that there will be no availability for either party to abandon post-integration because they both have as much to lose.

The problem with this method is that the integration, or intimacy, will be questioned at every interval to scout out the balance of exchange. Never will there be a case of true romantic intimacy and coinciding vulnerability because the pre-integration exchange will defuse what would be high levels of existential integration. This is due to the universal nature of existential integration. An individual is only able to existentially integrate from a universal or general standpoint, since the individualist details become too excessive, which does not allow a smooth integration. The more singular the individual postulates themselves, the less available they are for integration, which is to de-individualize the person in entirety.

The issue with intimacy without a balanced exchange is that an individual may become existentially disoriented following integration. The hope is that their compensation, which involves the proponent who contains the intimacy post-integration, accounts for all the subsidiaries that made intimacy possible. In this way, when they offer advanced conscious substance, they will surpass themselves until they embody most of the intimacy.

We are already noticing a pattern, which explains why monetary exchange diverts our attention from the occasion. By having a method of exchange agreed upon by all, we presume that the value of exchange offsets the existential loss post-integration. As it appears, the individual is selling their existential self, and is perceived as a respite from the loss of the existential self—post-intimacy.

Yet this is not a case of *selling* oneself, for there is a genuine objective: to follow the conscious seed through existential offering until one becomes more than they are, or is respected for what they are already. The monetary exchange is not an antidote but a diversion from the realized experience.

The difficulty with this approach is that we heavily rely on the conscious proponents to recognize the existential offerings that enabled the intimacy, especially when there is a diversion via monetary exchange, which might lead the individual to believe that debts are settled through the market. Mere recognition is insufficient, as the subsidiaries are seeking a conscious offering.

According to the degree of existential offering, there should be a balanced conscious spillover. When those who have existentially offered are unwilling to permit the conscious spillover, they become disruptive within the system. They result in offering themselves for monetary compensation, even though the dynamic is not centered on market exchange, but rather on existential exchange.

The system's aversion to connection-based exchange stems from individuals becoming increasingly individualistic, compelled to operate within the rigid structures of normative dynamics. They cannot access the shared pot of consciousness to absorb its contents, as they begin to question who brought forth the conscious material and why it is relevant to them, especially in terms of what they are existentially risking.

Highly conscious proponents typically do not risk as much existentially, as they rely on others for their development. The primary aspects applicable to them are their own existential selves, which can be integrated for further conscious development or, ultimately, for intimacy.

Intimacy, as stated, is conscious substance that becomes existentially grounded. It partakes in a particular conscious substance which, in full utilization, forms the basis for conscious development. However, because the criteria that lead to intimacy are restricted, it only incorporates conscious material that meets those criteria.

For instance, religious identity is a form of intimacy for conscious substance, but it always falls short of encompassing the full conscious experience because it is tied to specific identity parameters. Childhood familial bonds are another example of restricted intimacy, as they provide an intimate share limited to those early life experiences. Romantic intimacy in the present moment is notable for encompassing much of the psyche's conscious material, unless it fails to interact with the universal environment. This might occur if the romance is arranged, identity-bound, family-bound, or otherwise environmentally limited.

There are instances in which one accesses higher conscious realms through states of loss and mourning. Loss occurs when one cannot tolerate the intrusion of consciousness due to a lack of contextual layers necessary to engage with it. This leads to an internal collapse, wherein the lower states of consciousness are overwhelmed by the demands of the external environment.

The depressive state is the voice of these lower conscious realms trying to assert themselves. Depression arises not simply from loss but from the ongoing struggle to persist amid overwhelming forces, all without success. This dynamic, refusing to decline while being subjected to a force that supersedes and negates relevance, results in a state of continual motion. Hence, the symptom is one of persistent depression, as no resolution is achieved. Resolution comes only through either a consensual acceptance of decline or the provision of an expanded context in which to engage, rather than being forced into passive irrelevance.

To create this expanded context, one must be above the situation, perceiving it from a third-party perspective. When genuine interaction occurs, each proponent must hold enough context to view the situation neutrally, enabling them to extract and distill information according to their individual needs. This requires multiple interaction gates that protect their personal existential realm from overload.

71

Exchange of Existential Material

This same paradox emerges even when interactions appear indistinguishable. While most conceptual material can be distinguished through relational factors, existential material yields no insight for a final selection. For instance, when we perceive the interaction of two people, there will always be subtle distinctions in their interactions. We can analyze most experiences by breaking them into parts, but raw existential experience resists matching specific relational content, unique and available for distinct intellectual analysis. However, the interaction with conscious substance, or existential material, cannot be analyzed for specificity in a way that proves it to be more than its degree. While we could study interaction with specific conscious material, we cannot understand its mode of consciousness other than by noting its degree by contrast to others.

An imposing mistake is made when we assume that degree can be defined by conscious substance alone or by existential material alone. A conscious substance without existential material might be presumed high-degree for some reason; yet only existential material defines the true degree. The other factor is practiced intimacy, which grounds conscious material in the existential realm. Intimacy is the footing of existential material mediated through the biological domain. The cost of intimacy is supplementary existential material, absorbed by those components already containing it in the intense existential sphere. For instance, sharing a meal can be a form of intimacy; the act of consuming food allows another realm to absorb the existential material gained from that exchange. The degree of intimacy corresponds to the existential capacity carried by the rest of the system.

We can perceive intimacy as a method of ingesting conceptual material via human, animal, or plant reserves. Even so, intimacy remains a conceptualization at the adjoining point on the line dividing the biological and conceptual selves. The appearance of transfer through high levels of intimacy is merely the highest degree of effect, which makes it appear as a true bridging; although in the essential realm there will never be an actual transfer between the two. Therefore, as fortunate as intimacy seems, it does not solve the problem but merely defers it. The existential capacity is real only because of the transfer of consciousness. When the server has served the consumer, the transfer of intimacy appears as an interface, while the real exchange is the transfer of conscious substance that brought the intimacy to bear.

We could prove this by having the server provide service from a distance, which would still be an exchange of intimacy but not of consciousness. If the reader is not satisfied, consider that speech, first and foremost, and physical expression, second, will transfer existential material. That material is always the result of conscious substance, never a standalone entity to be experienced. We cannot find a novice of limited conscious and intellectual range who is nevertheless riddled with existential material.

To interact with a conscious substance that bears any degree of existential material, or, more precisely, to engage with existential material as if it contains something more appealing, is identical whether the substance is declining or progressive. The choice to engage becomes paradoxical as well, for there is no rationale to prefer one formation of existential material over another. The only distinguishing factor is the degree of that material.

We can deduce, without direct evidence, that the degree of existential material corresponds to the grandiosity of the conscious or universal substance. There is no confirmation because we do not possess an exact account of the connection between existential and conscious materials. They work together, the conceptual and biological aspects of human experience hand in hand. The conceptualization is the conscious material, since consciousness is purely conceptual. The existential material is the felt experience of the biological self when disparity arises between conceptual formation and pure selfhood.

Ideally, there would be no existential material, for the conceptual realm would be integrated into the biological one. Yet achieving such perfection is impossible because the realms are not biologically linked, at least according to a biological perception. We may theorize their linkage but cannot resolve it under biological rules, which do not fully acknowledge the conceptual realm as part of the organism.

Simulated Contexts and the Relatability Complex

One is naturally endowed with a relatability complex, to which they are immediately subjected to the self-referential nature of existing relationships, whether it is with current social beings, the environment, or in reflection with selfhood. Reflection of selfhood, in this case, refers to the constitution of one's abridged view of the framework and proportion of a surrounding relatability metric. One never truly loves or hates themselves; rather, in contrast to a scenario of relatability, they do so. It is self-referential in order to gain more access to what is external.

When someone lacks the contextual understanding of the forms of intimacy they engage in, operating at a level where they merge with what they connect to and cannot intellectually define the nature of that connection; it is the connection itself they experience, not its meaning. If this connection is immediate and without contextual separation (even though such separations will eventually arise), it indicates a lack of intellectual sentience in that regard.

The endowment of relatability initiates a rehearsal of whatever criteria have been impacted by this form of connection. In other words, the entire sequence becomes relatable, not as a perfectly unified whole, but precisely at the points where the self detached to facilitate that unification. Therefore, if the object is before us, its sub-structural relatability lies in how it reflects back upon the aspects of individuality we mislaid to enable that connection. A strong connection thus facilitates an innate relatability to its reversal, allowing one to experience oneself in the loss of attributes that made the connection possible, through that very connection.

When we speak of connection, we refer to the empathetic attachment of oneself to an aspect, phenomenon, environment, or person. Without context, this connection leads to a relatability with the adversarial element and a negation of selfhood that further facilitates it.

The primary connection one partakes is often parental figures. This attachment, when formed without context from either party, and thus unexpected by the child, produces, through the union, a relatability to the adverse effects or loss of personhood that made the relationship possible. This is the common pathos of parental figures: they resent or feel disproportionate sentimentality toward their children in the recognition of their own vulnerabilities. They instinctively relate to their child through the adversarial quantification that necessitated the bond; then endure emotional turmoil when confronting their own fragility.

Although all relationships are fundamentally based on the attachment of vulnerability, their relatability, at least in its innate form, does not aim to represent the adversarial elements that underlie them, because the bond itself is not aligned with that agenda. Typical relational material carries contextual elements that introduce intellectual awareness, preventing the level of bondage that would cause innate relatability to emphasize adversarial loss.

This dynamic creates codependency: when relatability becomes tied to an adversarial aspect of one's personhood, one must remain attached to the unification in order to preserve the status quo. Innate relatability remains latent in both substance and materiality. Although constant throughout the relationship, at the point of codependency, security is measured by the balance provided through the object of connection. Despite the adversarial element which subconsciously incurs significant psychic expenditure, the benefits of the attachment parallel and justify its continuation.

In other words, although innate relatability is corrupted by adversarial dynamics, the experience of connection is structured in a way that softens one's psyche and renders it available to another psyche that does not endure the same adversity. In this way, a symbiotic relationship is exemplified in its strictest form.

Innate relatability differs from general relatability in that it represents the subconscious baseline of connection, unaffected by more developed theories or conscious experiences of relatability. Just as the general relatability of a child to a parent is one of love or positivity, innate relatability can encompass adversarial elements. The adversarial element measures the psychic expenditure required for that depth of unification. Without a deep connection, there can be no ascendancy of the adversarial element.

For example, a child who has never met their parent may manifest an adversarial narrative, as if rehearsing abandonment or disengagement, even though this is not an expression of innate relatability. In fact, the opposite is true: the innate relatability toward the absent parent remains positive and connecting, since there was never a genuine bond to fracture. The general relatability, what society or politics assigns to the individual, is adversarial because communal empathy deems abandonment the appropriate interpretation.

Despite the material presence of the object, our concern lies not with that materiality but with the connection between psyche and object. We often encounter negative material, such as an abandoned father, who nonetheless retains innate relatability due to the absence of an actual bond. No amount of demonization can create adversarial relatability where bondage ever existed.

The adversarial element in relatability can only arise from the level of connection to which one directs attention. It can emerge toward an object oblivious to one's existence, or even a construct lacking individuality. Yet, because relatability overrides psychotonomy, it transforms into adversariality by disrupting a part of the psyche. Thus, the primary axiom applies: you can only hate what you love. Bondage must precede adversarial relatability, and yet the adversarial element remains arbitrary to the object's material or intrinsic qualities.

Consider the father who abandoned his child: this act is judged negative by communal moral standards, but it does not elicit innate adversarial relatability, only because there was no distinct connection to begin with. Conversely, an overbearing parent can create intense bondage for which adversarial sentiment arises, despite societal norms viewing excessive affection as wholly positive.

This insight dispels the notion that attachment to perfected personas or ideal objects is necessary; rather, it is the level of connection that matters. One can experience innate relatability even through detrimental examples, provided the bondage is not profound.

This framework explains how parts of selfhood appear neglected. Psychology often interprets such neglect as deliberate choice, creating fragmentation within the self. While this model holds for objective systems, where focusing on one component neglects another, the psyche does not function in isolation. It is inherently inclusive; it does not ignore parts even when emphasis shifts.

If one intensely centers on a specific aspect, the psyche naturally allows innate relatability toward the remaining parts, retrieving comprehensive information of the whole system. Whether one inhabits a discipline, institution, or any contained environment, whether internal or external, they will reflect backward so innate relatability includes information not presently included.

For example, if one is in an institution far removed from their family of origin, we cannot say that the institution provides the same habitat. Still, through innate relatability, the entire institutional structure helps relate back to earlier mental frameworks, allowing the whole psyche to be included in that institutional experience. The psyche has no reason to separate these domains. Even though the institution is distinct and represents a new phase, it functions only within contextual criteria. One phase is one phase; the other is another. But in terms of relatability, the innate structure does not engage with the individual's conscious choices or psychic overlay; rather, it operates as an intrinsic process, doing whatever is necessary to reflect back within the psyche.

This process gives the illusion of neglecting parts of selfhood. In reality, it manifests as an adversarial representation within the relatability complex. We respond to one domain in reference to a prior domain but do so adversarially, as if attacking a neglected part of the psyche due to a failure of general relatability.

At no point is there absolute neglect of selfhood's parts. Instead, the relatability complex casts adversarial connotations onto a facet of the psyche, exposing its vulnerability. In every interaction, internal or external, two types of connection occur: by contrast and by unification. Normally, parts of the psyche connect through unification, but here they connect via vulnerability, enabling distant connections.

For instance, to connect with a distant cousin without an established bond, one either follows their lineage back toward immediate family, using that connection as a bridge, or one follows the cousin's vulnerability as a contrast to the family bond. In the latter case, connection depends on vulnerability despite the distance.

This phenomenon is psychic distance. When one fixates on one domain, a "relatability complex" arises, pointing to a visceral vulnerability in a prior part of the psyche that is not present in the current domain. The connection persists but is weakened. Unlike external mechanisms, this internal process anxiously expresses conflicts between parts of the self or simulates interpersonal connections when they are absent. Because it lacks the mutual, interlocking experience of two individuals, its emotional impact is less critical than genuine interpersonal conflict.

Collapse of Intimacy in Degenerated Environments

In the desolate tract-conscious environment, the appropriate approach is to avoid anything needing contextual justification and focus solely on biological necessities. For instance, choosing the nearest market out of geographical proximity, because it satisfies a biological necessity. The biological importance will imbue the action as a manifestation of the organism and will not incorporate a contextual layer. Another example is bathing, which is a certain biological necessity but can be used in a more well-appointed manner. A third example can be sexual relations which can be stimulated as would the organism in its sexual demand or through sexual fantasy and contemplation.

This could be for the purpose that it is assumed that if normalization occurs, through repeated, unconscious reactions, then the individual system is capable of surviving without existential intuition, as seen in the case of warriors or medical personnel.

The vagabond, however, does not understand the notion that these biological needs are vulnerable to personhood, as they have come to accept a life where biological needs are momentary and futile. Vagabonds endure hunger and sleepless nights until these conditions no longer feel urgent. In other words, once deprivation is normalized, the crisis of need disappears; instead, biological vulnerability will be left to life-and-death experiences or major psyche complexes, such as those imprinted from childhood. In the case of a warrior, they too become adapted to the situation of life and death and lose the sense of their vulnerability, accepting death at any moment. For them, that life scenario does not create a sense of biological vulnerability and thus will lose the possibility of conscious grounding or intimacy.

We are beginning to grasp the core of the issue: even vagabonds face limitations in their biological vulnerability due to their eventual acceptance of their nature. As a result, they lose their sense of intimacy with any contextual access because their vagabond lifestyle prevents them from experiencing the biological sentiment in a meaningful way. This is why the vagabond lifestyle, as a path to continuous intimacy, is ultimately futile; it leads to the creation of a persona that has accepted the idea that humans must conform to biological needs molded by their environment.

Such a person does not find any regard for biological experience and will lose stability in their biological activity. They will not understand the difference between eating out of the waste set against normal social ingestion. Biological need is the same in a garbage heap as in a fine eating place, and they do not place themselves as advocates for choosing the situation, as per the accepted environment despite its variability. In this sense, the vagabond will eventually lose their sociability because the biological needs will be accessed without any deliberation, and this in turn will lose their civilized connection which will degrade their conscious activity and contextual normality.

Nexus and Desolate Tract Environments

In terms of the environment, there are two types worthy of discussion at the moment. One environment can be considered a nexus of conscious manifestation, and the other, a desolate tract of conscious exposition. These environments are not considered in terms of residence or housing but rather as overarching political or existential structures.

In the conscious environment, biological activity is attached to the exposition of consciousness, including the specificity of smaller environments within that structure. In contrast, within the desolate tract of consciousness, biological activity is not attached to any overarching system and is only connected to personhood's existential material. When intimacy is sought out in a conscious desolate tract, one loses environmental consciousness and becomes a desolate tract; just like the chosen attachment. For the overarching environment is always the dominant conscious force, regardless of individualistic traits.

Thus, in the desolate tract-like environment, the final manifestation of intimacy will also be desolate tract-like, for that is the embodied structure. However, there is no inherent problem with biological activity in the desolate tract, as long as no active conscious intimacy is sought through existential availability. In the case of the nexus of consciousness, the environment constantly exposes with contextual additives that far surpass individualistic depth. Therefore, any biological activity under its umbrella will inevitably take part in that exposition.

Even without existential availability, or even within continuous contextual frameworks, intimacy will not be halted. The consciousness of the nexus supersedes whatever limited contextual information may disclose within the individual. The shallow individual, lacking existential availability, is still not protected from accessing it because the nexus's consciousness compels self-consciousness.

The desolate tract of consciousness becomes a safe habitat for continuous biological activities that occur without conscious intention do not lead to intimacy. This is especially true when one is not consciously deliberating on their existential self, or when one partakes in a contextual layer that automatically transcends the desolate tract-like status of the environment. They will not be compelled to engage, this includes even consciously available individuals, because the desolate tract does not impose itself upon anyone.

The only problem arises with biological activity that is not chastely biological, but presumes an existential or contextual meaning. For instance, when someone seeks out an environment within the desolate tract that is not necessary, it requires contextual justification. Any action requiring contextual justification becomes problematic in a desolate tract-consciousness environment. Conversely, any biological activity in the nexus of consciousness can be questioned, for it automatically engages in a form of intimacy.

Thus, normal activity within the nexus involves conscious awareness of biological activity across various environments. This ensures participation in the wholeness of consciousness, rather than in the privatization or isolation that comes with strong identities.

Vagabond: Degradation and Redemption

The only way the vagabond can maintain continuity without degradation is by becoming aware of this process; by momentarily rediscovering their biological vulnerability and accepting hospitality to restore their sensibilities. In order for vagabonds to sustain themselves, they must continuously cycle through experiences of biological vulnerability without fully surrendering to environmental determinism.

To better understand the cycle of degradation, we can follow its stages:

Stage One: The vagabond experiences biological vulnerability, feeling a sense of dependency and psychological demand for a specific biological need.

Stage Two: After an interval of constant biological vulnerability and then fulfillment, they move toward the next stage. With such an arduous process of vulnerability, eventually the psyche begins to accept that the regular sociality of personhood should not interfere with biological necessity.

Stage Three: Whatever the biological necessities require, however or whenever the needs are fulfilled, is not a matter of personhood but is solely based on the momentary movements of existence.

In this stage, they begin to lose sensitivity in playing an active role in fulfilling biological needs. They no longer view sustenance as something a person seeks, but rather as a process in which sustenance either comes or does not. They see themselves as detached from that process, observing it as a third-party. When their stomach demands food, they do not respond by actively seeking it out. Instead, they experience hunger pangs as if they were external phenomena, unrelated to themselves and their identity. The degree to which hunger is perceived as an externality reflects the extent of degradation of their personhood. In the extreme case, the hunger pangs feel so distant from the self that fulfilling them becomes akin to feeding a stranger.

Simulation and Breakdown of Intimacy

This leads us from the individual's cycle of degradation to a more collective understanding; how locations themselves can simulate or suppress intimacy when contextual vitality is lost. The interactive locale is sustained by a specific structure of consciousness; if this structure is disrupted, the outcome deteriorates. Its viability depends on the presence of consciousness capable of engagement; just as evocative interaction with a person requires their active presence and receptivity.

When attempting to engage with someone who is unavailable, two outcomes may arise. First, through persistent effort or protestation, the other may become responsive, recognizing and reciprocating the interactive experience. Second, if no response is forthcoming, the initiator may continue alone, eventually constructing an imagined framework around the other; a social proxy designed to be operable in their absence. This trait is common, where compelled interaction requires both parties to participate in an existential formation of sociality, thereby binding them. In this way, one gains control through a coerced dynamic.

A similar process unfolds within the psyche in relation to sociality. Even without external interaction, the mind can persist in imagined engagement, until, at some point, a simulated counterpart emerges and begins to respond in kind. This intentionality is crucial for forming imaginative responses. Once the individual takes control of the simulation, they can reshape the perceived response into a receptive one. When the simulation provides interaction, the individual can repurpose that interaction for aims less rooted in existential engagement: validation replaces dynamic relational exchange. The more controlled the perceived interaction, the less existential-weight it carries, measured against the internal database that constitutes a person's self-concept.

In future reengagements, prior internal developments may be lost if the perceptual framework registers no change. The interaction resumes where it left off, even if intellectual growth has transpired. Although simulations can still shape criteria for real interaction, this can lead to dissonance, expecting a new dynamic when no existential change has actually taken place.

When consciousness descends from an "all-access" state, unbound by context or structure, into a situated, embodied state, its availability becomes dependent on those structures. All-access consciousness (a psychological state where normal filters and boundaries dissolve, allowing complete exposure to internal and external stimuli) exists beyond specific contexts and can be likened to a child encountering pornography: the content reaches without a contextual filter. The child approaches not out of directed interest but because no binding structure mediates the experience. The issue lies not in the pornography itself, but in the child's inability to contextualize, resulting in unfiltered access to a domain removed from social organization.

Two conditions enable all-access consciousness: structural removal and non-contextual interaction. If the pornographic construct had not stripped away the social structure of sexuality, direct interaction, consequences, and existential weight, or if the child had the maturity to contextualize the experience as one might with art, this kind of unfiltered consciousness would not occur.

Consciousness becomes accessible through two key elements: sociality and structurality, the latter a manifestation of the former. Normally, consciousness, and its value in relational exchange, is anchored in sociality. For example, a family unit represents a composite consciousness shaped by the social dynamics of its members. Each member holds a key to that spectrum, and when one is absent, the family's consciousness remains incomplete.

The exchange among members supports the development of that consciousness, and without interaction, it stagnates until exchange resumes. In this context, parental figures occupy the highest level of exchange for consciousness, with siblings providing regulation. Thus, social exchange follows a hierarchy and contains consciousness within each member, forming a full system. We regard the family as a whole, abstracting from its real-world position to consider it as a complete perspective. The family's sociality is embedded in each member and also reflected in structural elements, namely, the home and possessions. Every mental association with the unit exemplifies its sociality. This is the typical situation.

However, the family unit can become dismembered from its structural and social organization when members partake in opportunities that mimic the familial experience conceptually, either within the psyche or externally, outside the family's influence. In this case, sociality fractures into conceptual interactions that no longer align with a coherent spectrum. The family's composite consciousness is no longer available for all-access within the unit, and its social organization may even be forgotten. This development can protect each member from unrelenting familial exposure, interaction without context would otherwise be permeable to an extreme degree.

Therefore, the dismembering of consciousness from its sociality is made possible when developments of the spectrum are enacted in a conceptual form for the constituents that make up that organization. Now, we have a sociality that is not organized solely by direct existential engagement and the exchange of consciousness within a rigid hierarchy; rather, sociality both engages existentially and simultaneously develops conceptually beyond or outside that immediate exchange. This is not a problem, only an outcome, to which pronounced sociality differs from individualized conceptual development.

In the case of locality, it requires its structural removal, something that, under normal circumstances, is deeply entwined with every existential and social aspect involved in its formation, and remains inaccessible without ascending the ladder of sociality and existential risk. Secondly, if a locality exists without context, that is, without regulating frameworks to filter perception, then that locality becomes exposed to all-access consciousness. In such spaces, the psyche receives input without interruption or interpretive framing.

Those two elements cause over-exposure but are also prerequisites for an interactive locale. When consciousness is bound to structure, it cannot be engaged without taking structural, social, and existential risks, and, importantly, without creating another locale capable of such engagement. The only way to address the first element while maintaining a coherent interactive locale is by remaining unbound to its structural organization or sociality, placing it, in a sense, in a desolate tract where interaction with consciousness is not limited by structural separation because no new structure exists to create such separation.

The second element, namely context, is only accessible when all-access consciousness is available. Even within its own locale, one requires context to access it. In a different locale, this necessitates referencing context back to the original source; a cumbersome process, especially within a complex organization. Moreover, since this element does not interact directly with consciousness but only through the context by which consciousness is engaged, the individuals within that locality must be psychically revitalized through mobility to reach a stage where they can extend their context beyond the immediate sphere of influence.

Context layered upon context cannot be sustained over ordinary time due to its inherent complexity. The psyche can interact only at a single point, not with a point that refers to another point. If, at any moment, the locality treats these as the same context within existential sociality, it risks creating a new form of consciousness that merely simulates the real one; thus, attempts to engage meaningfully will ultimately fail. Therefore, context must remain distinct from genuine contextual formation, so that at this secondary level it is constructed on thin air, demanding not only a barren material foundation but also an equally desolate conceptual framework.

However, the embodied interactive locale, where interactivity is divorced from consciousness attachment, structurally, socially, or physically, operates on an internal context innate to its design and not directly linked to consciousness sentiment. Such a locale can exist even in non-access consciousness because it never relied on consciousness to begin with; it functions through the memory traces of its participants, removed upon their departure. Consciousness changes pose no threat, as the construction differs fundamentally from direct attribution to consciousness. In fact, maintaining an interactive embodied locale under all-access consciousness is more difficult, like surrounding it with pornography. Separating such a locale requires rigid formation and internal context.

Examples of interactive embodied locales include prisons and museums. A prison, lacking a clearly adhered internal context, is separated from direct interaction with consciousness. As a result, the process of cultivation differs fundamentally from that outside it, since they exist within an interactive, embodied loop of development.

Naturally, if a proper individualized or general context were present, the locale itself would transform, but that is not the focus here. In contrast, a museum maintains a very strict internal context while still retaining some access to what lies beyond its boundaries. It therefore qualifies as an interactive embodied locale. Museums operate predominantly within a modality of non-access consciousness and tend to deteriorate under conditions of all-access consciousness. For instance, if "pornography" is right outside its walls, how can a nude figure inside be regarded as art? Conversely, if the possibility of consciousness is not triggered simply by the street corner, then an entirely new concept of art would arise, one that neither interacts with nor is influenced by the external environment. This is because external access occurs through context alone, rather than through direct experience.

Intimacy and the Familial Loop

The familial circle is considered a consciousness musing and by a default degree of association causes personhood to presume the entirety of their consciousness to be kept up with that surrounding. We must agree that the familial enterprise, although reflects a degree of consciousness, does not enjoin with the ultimate degree nor to the substantiated level of personhood.

We can analogize this as two locales of structural consciousness, namely the consciousness center and its satellite mirrors of that entity. When enduring a satellite locale, which does entail a whole criteria of degrees, there is a stipulation to be absent from intimate engagements. As we have defined intimacy as the bridge of consciousness, by having such an event under a satellite locale, causing wholesome personhood to be amassed in the presumed conscious exposition. This would cause personhood to become the mirror which is destined to reflect but owing to the entire embodiment it does not reflect for such is the center of existence. The same can be said for the familial junction, consciousness that is processed in its center organization is only an abridgement of the social rumination which is further bound to the definite center wherever it is located.

When the familial body is situated in near proximity to the consciousness center then it does not retain the dread of misfortune. Because it can never be presumed to be more than a mirror upon consciousness, as consciousness contemplates beyond the front door, it can never be presumed to be the actual center. Although, in the rare case of cult-like behavior, it may be separated from the consciousness exposition with certain success. The further the familial junction is from the consciousness exposition, the more dreadful it becomes as a presumed center.

In fact, nothing else can be done other than to presume such, for there is no other conscious exposition on par with structural consciousness. The familial junction will naturally become an assumed proprietary domain of consciousness because it is a domain set apart from structural consciousness. There are elements that correct this course, although this is the natural inclination of the familial body that performs on the periphery of structural consciousness.

Let us be clear: personhood is inherently privy to all intimacy, serving as the basis for the emergence of a higher degree of selfhood. Intimacy endures despite the warrants of the subjects, and this is because we are constantly seeking a consciousness endeavor. Technically, there is no reason a domain should be constructed external to the periphery of structural consciousness because the entire enterprise of elements is deeply dependent on the structural center.

When we construct a domain on the periphery of structural consciousness, we do so with the understanding that it mirrors structural consciousness and serves as a locale; both distant enough for third-party observation and near enough for representation, all for the illusion of being part of that system. The familial domain will come to be presumed as the entirety of consciousness, prompting each member to transfer that intimacy according to the consciousness of that locale. This locale does not distinguish itself as a consciousness of its own but rather mirrors a reflection at any corner of its system. Therefore, we will approach the subject of elements that defer this natural inclination toward the decadence of the familial body in such a locale.

Interaction, Intimacy, and Codependency in Dynamics

We find an intersection of three elements: interaction, intimacy, and codependency. It is fair to say that when there is complete interaction, there is no capacity for intimacy. Intimacy is the bond between two components that are not relegated through interaction. They attach for a variety of reasons, so the reverse clause, that non-interactions are necessarily intimate, is false. The reason for intimacy varies, but for this discussion, interaction refers to relationship material connecting two components and relegated to the interactive realm, which is unavailable for the closeness intimacy requires. There is proximity between interactive material, yet that is only adjudged in respect to the elements that prove its interaction, something purely subjective. The object of interaction is merely the cause of the interactive manifestation and can be seen only as the effect of a certainty for one's subjective experience.

Intimacy, on the other hand, involves wholesome elements not based on subjective material. There may be little reason for the attachment, but by the mere experience of intimacy, the two elements bond. It is as if intimacy is a tool of connection residing outside subjective possibility. This tool can emerge outside the realm of familiarity and often ascends between elements that would not bond otherwise; for there is no familiarity or interactive material to connect them.

We can assert a second clause: yesterday's intimacy is today's interaction. The bond relegated to intimacy is such with objective agreement but not subjective. The individual partakes in intimacy even amidst the odds of subjective material. Eventually, that material seeks justification of the bond by revealing interactive material to make familiar what has already been juxtaposed into the psyche, as if the neighbor has already been chosen without adjudication in which one must find familiarity with that proximity.

When preliminary intimacy remains in its original position, without interactive apparatus joining to find familiarity with the connection, the individual is compelled to repeat that connection and presume it the high point of their advancement. Intimacy, by its default system, relegates the linkage commencing from personhood with elements so advanced that familiarity is not possible. This is not the meaning of intimacy itself, but only a manifestation of its system as arbitrator for elements without the ability to connect. The objective of intimacy is the natural mode of operation when connection is sought without interactive material, regardless of the object of interest.

Therefore, a problematic instance arises: an object of intimacy may be of little substance, yet the effect of that connection, lacking interactive material, leads the psyche to presume that the prevalence of the entire system adheres to that entity. For instance, a long-term relationship can develop intimacy, which then causes individuals to presume their counterpart as the entity most worthy of interaction, thereby diminishing their growth. This can be seen as a perpetual, cyclical growth span: individuals develop, regard their connection with intimacy, then dispose of that growth to pursue the interaction as their highest regard.

We may wonder about the possibility of intimacy over the duration of a relationship, and that depends on its process. If the incoming intimacy is newfound, the experience aligns with the existential makeup of the present moment. To have newfound intimacy at regular intervals requires an existential separation, which effectively removes all familiar attachments.

This means that if a complete interaction endures the relationship, there is no possibility for intimacy; conversely, intimacy manifests in a retrogressive manner. Without adhering to a codex of existential separation, a highly interactive relationship is privy to an intimacy experience that causes individuals to lose their ground and regress to the dormant existential platform. Whatever stage they were in at that time becomes the moment of regression.

Comparable to the parent-child relationship, where intimacy is unexpected but, when it occurs, may cause the parent to lose stability and regress to their childhood existential reality. This is not to dismiss intimacy in that setting, for after existential separation, the enduring intimacy between parent and child is newfound and unlikely to cause the parent to retrogress into their childhood state. Just as a stranger experiencing intimacy with a child would likely result in an awkward encounter, since the child represents universal elements rather than their own existential makeup.

We arrive at a third clause: the manner of interaction determines the existential bond for the intimate outcome. When encountering a famous person, the embedded interactive material, all relating to universal elements (i.e., fame), causes the intimate manifestation to be universally related and not threaten regression.

When interaction is universally related, existential attachment manifests as a current endowment of one's existential reach into a universal realm grander than personhood. For example, the family dynamic may be interpreted as representing universal elements (e.g., the child as a masculine or feminine symbol or generational representation). In such cases, intimacy endured with family members aligns with universal elements rather than the familiar, personal elements that the child represents in their existential makeup.

Universal representation falls short in accounting for interactive material that continues to offer potential advantages. While the family dynamic reflects universal aspects, the personal biological reflection that is most powerful within it remains inaccessible through interaction. This is why it is most beneficial to engage from a parent-to-child perspective in environments that offer insights into personal foundations and meaningful topics. When intimacy persists, interactions provide sufficient data points to prevent regression into the existential state of childhood. Though such intimacy may not offer the protective edge of broad universal themes, it is enough to sustain the mature aspects of parenting and the vulnerability of childhood.

However, because familiarity stems from interactive material, it may limit the emergence of further intimate opportunities to "settle the score." As interactions become overly familiar and variable, the cycle ceases to be intimate but as something else entirely. Intimacy, in this context, is the horizon of attachment, available only to unanticipated capabilities. In contrast, interaction comprises the most familiar elements of personhood, making true intimacy unlikely, though it increases the likelihood of biological reflection or present understanding. Long-term ritualized relationships centered on interactive material may either regress to childhood bonds or maintain a surface-level engagement that fails to endure. Such interactions may suppress the reemergence of childhood interactive states but cannot provide a sanctuary for the familial representation of universal implication. Instead, it reflects singularity, with each family member contributing only in accordance with their role in one's current existential makeup.

The universal realm remains inaccessible within familial interaction unless the interaction itself allows universal elements to be explored. In these cases, the interaction is no longer just an exchange of interactive material, it becomes a top-down process where universal elements guide the engagement rather than being determined by it. When this occurs, the interaction becomes more universal and thus more open to intimacy and its latent potential.

When a relationship relies exclusively on one component, namely interactive material, it becomes a representation of childhood bonds. This often leads to a simplistic regression or, at worst, a childlike orientation. Conversely, an intimate bond characterized by continuous novelty depends entirely on the evolving diversity of each individual. In such cases, intimacy reaches the other extreme, producing an existential bond where roles reverse: the parent becomes the child, the child becomes the parent, and spouses become each other's existential mirrors. This mediation arises only when intimate bonds are formed without interactive material which supports a broader conversation. Without the buffering effect of familiarity, the relationship resembles two unrelated species unable to form a shared habitat.

Thus, both extremes, intimacy devoid of interactive potential and interaction devoid of intimate potential, lead to either existential regression or stagnation. Both invoke infantile dynamics, but extreme intimacy transforms this into an existential state.

In situations of existential separation, where future interaction cultivates intimacy as a current and universal experience, one caveat remains: if the interactive material remains unchanged from past to present, then despite the existential shift creating a seemingly new reality, prior mental imagery rooted in old interactions will resurface. This differs from encounters with strangers, where interactions are intimate and current precisely because no shared prior-interactive-material exists. There's no reason to assume that interaction draws from dormant aspects of personhood or infantile components, for being that it represents a novel experience it would extract ones.

In familiar relationships, even after existential separation, interaction inevitably regresses to previous states. Therefore, both a refresh of interactive material and a genuine existential separation are required to experience another person as a "stranger" with present-time diversity and universality.

Natural interactive material always manifests as the most approximating elements of personhood that encounter the least resistance. If one does not evolve their interactive material, relationships will stagnate in familiar and infantile dynamics, such as maternal or paternal bonds and other early-life frameworks. This eventually leads to a stalemate, with both individuals feeling drained as the interaction revolves around outdated or irrelevant elements. Without external input to evolve interactive material, it withers, especially in adulthood, which seeks more expansive and universal experiences. The only way to sustain this material is to introduce external influences that allow the relationship to evolve toward a new horizon.

This explains why highly interactive relationships are often adjacent to universal elements or external influences, their continuity relies on such influences, even if the relationship itself appears stable. These dependencies may not be fully acknowledged within the relationship but serve a crucial function by providing the necessary structure to sustain interaction. Rather than projecting universal sentiment onto the relationship itself, such individuals locate universal elements outside the relationship, maintaining such externally while continuing their interactive experience.

Conversely, when relationships lack substantial interactive material, intimacy seeks external sources to compensate. Individuals may align themselves with highly interactive figures or contexts to draw in external influences that maintain universal continuity and prevent regression. This makes it possible to engage in both interactive material and existential separation, allowing intimacy to lead to personal evolution without relapse.

Still, it is common for people to rely on external dependencies to complete this process. For example, aristocratic societies, as centers of high consciousness, often define relationships primarily through the external interactive material that influences personal connections. This compensates for an inability to sustain intimacy without reverting to familiar interactive narratives. Likewise, in lower or inconsequential social structures, where constant interaction occurs, external elements provide a universal imprint that breaks cycles of repetition, enabling intimacy to evolve.

Codependency emerges most clearly when intimacy lacks both interactive material and existential separation. Without new interactive input, interaction recycles stale dynamics and emotional states which are tied to them. This alone doesn't produce codependency, but when intimacy is introduced into this stagnant space, the bond between two individuals becomes so entangled that individuality dissolves. Subjective experience deteriorates as the counterpart "downloads" unto the self, with no renewed interactive material to contextualize or understand the relationship. Without new lenses for perception, intimacy becomes totalizing, an all-consuming experience that disregards subjectivity and variation. If interactive material had evolved, even deep intimacy could retain novelty, preserving personal perspectives and preventing codependency.

Yet this risk centers on the absence of existential separation. When such separation does occur, it resets the dynamic, reintroducing the individual as a stranger, unburdened by previous emotional downloads or habitual patterns.

On the other hand, in highly interactive dynamics, codependency is unlikely unless intimacy appears after interactive material has become irrelevant. This usually takes time, as relationships based on interactive exchange often pursue novelty. But when interaction becomes repetitive and insufficient for development, and intimacy emerges at that point, it creates a vacuum; no fertile interactive material and yet a strong emotional bond. This is the occasion of codependency.

Dynamics of Intimacy, Identity, and Political Influence

Intimacy localities are widespread, filling every corner and offering the most authentic experience of their unique sub-state. They seem unable to imagine any attachment beyond their immediate surroundings, claiming that their vitality comes from within their own core. However, despite this impression, these small localities are simply a contained expression of the entire country, or more specifically, the dominant contextual influence. It is said that their identity has generated certain feelings, which are stored in their traditional cultural "database."

These sources, which serve as evidence of intimate experience, are only discovered after the fact. Once these feelings have permeated the environment, intellectuals turn to the cultural "database" to trace their origins. There is a common belief that the logical process happened internally, because the sources, when examined within a specific context, become clear evidence.

The slight gap between the initial inspiration and those who later sought its source cannot be proven, as it is almost impossible to track. Another gap exists in individuals' emotional attachment to the source. Had they been aware of this connection, the true process might have been revealed. The reason this attachment often remains unnoticed is still an open question.

When intuition and honesty are present, influence extends beyond the boundaries of local distinctiveness, connecting to the larger political entity and its current cultural movements. These connections, which lead to a final attachment to this larger aspect, are hard to define logically. They might arise through something as simple as a street sign, the way someone speaks, or a change in local stores. What is clear is that they all ultimately trace back to an attachment to the political entity.

This is evident because anyone unwilling to accept that entity typically cannot engage with its cultural movements and, consequently, loses intimacy in whichever identity they embody. Any identity in conflict with the overarching political entity does not experience intimacy. This is not to say intimacy is impossible outside mainstream affiliations, but rather that dominant cultural frameworks often mediate what forms of intimacy are socially recognized or accessible. When intimacy does occur, it is because there is some degree of affection, even if negative, which allows a sense of cohesion within the identity.

The more an identity is at odds with the political establishment, the more negative the relationship will be, ensuring that some intimacy arises within their peculiar container. An identity under a political establishment cannot create distance without a particular charged relationship. The political entity, as the highest order, will always remain in dynamic with whatever lies underneath.

When an identity chooses to conflict with the political entity, it must adopt an adverse relationship, as non-relationship is not an option. This disapproval may appear negative in the political sphere, but for the identity in its intimacy, it serves as a strand of informational material that enhances that sense of intimacy, hence, positive in its final analysis.

Precisely because the structure of the political entity does not allow for an instinctive intimate experience, diminutive localities not only receive that intimate experience for themselves but also claim it as their origin. Such prerogative is understandable, as there is no reasonable alternative. With minimal effort and simple parameters of any identity, similar intimacy can manifest across a realm, even when the identities differ significantly.

These identities contain the entire interactive power of the state, since these mediums are necessary to interact with the state. Lacking a representative interactive structure of its own, the state cannot directly interact. An attempt to do so either results in nationalism or leads to a surplus of informational material with no relation to the individual. Vagrancy might be seen as a product of this material, in which the individual lacks a locality to interact with the state, thereby resulting in an overload of information. These individuals may be considered public personas, filled with too much of the state, lacking a mechanism to process or dilute that information, resulting in an erratic experience. When the content of their speech is transcribed, it reveals an entire database of current cultural information; though lacking coherence. This content proves immediately intrusive to the individual, as it contains the most applicable information, compelling engagement with the political entity.

Since the political entity constitutes a relationship that cannot be opted out of, there is a tendency to intuitively distance oneself from its current information, especially when comfort lies in prior material that the new information would displace, which would otherwise require engagement. The city becomes the habitat for those either willing to move to the next topic or who have relinquished autonomous interaction with information. An identity cannot reside in the heart of the city, as it cannot provide intimacy to each new encounter in a systematic way. It must remain on the periphery so that the present material does not disturb its intimacy, which remains attuned to a mature set of material.

This temporal disjunction may be referred to as the lag time between an identity's intimacy and the present set of cultural information from the political entity. The degree of lag correlates with the depth of intimacy. A deep intimacy within an identity will involve an outdated data set, even from a previous decade or century. A shallow intimacy will correspond to more recent memory.

An open question remains: can an identity work with a data set that is relatively close in time but evokes a deep intimate sense? Broadly speaking, this appears not to be the case. Yet, for the individual, can intimacy be experienced immediately after present material is introduced? This would require a process similar to that followed by an identity, executed without hindrance. Identity requires time to process new information among its constituents. It instinctively defends against inward information, still engaging with prior material.

Identity processes information by setting parameters and applying biological connections. It brings the information into proximity with the organic structure, integrating it as a part of its own flesh. Complete integration of all material is unfeasible, though the performance can be immediate. Time is required, as identity is cautious of systemic degradation. Individuals must consider what is applied to their organic structure and will generally avoid overloading the system.

When such overload occurs, the material is experienced as surface-level and lacks poetic depth. Overloading identity with present material causes a loss of conceptual potency. The identity ceases to function as a habitat for intimacy and begins to resemble a government institution, dense with political information, but incapable of offering intimacy. As a result, such institutions are often avoided, as they are localities that generate non-intimacy in all their interactions.

Individuals possess a mechanism for resisting excessive intimacy: a depletion of the entire apparatus that diminishes attachment to the psyche. This process prevents the imposition of intrusive material. Intimacy can only be experienced intermittently and with a limited number of selected informational elements. Any further attempts not only hinder meaningful interaction but also undermine the integrity of the entire intimate process.

Existential Attachment

When an individual is existentially attached to an object or construct, it becomes the dichotomy of their embodied existence in relation to an objective circumstance. Objective personification entails receiving the full existential nature of the individual, laid out upon a landscape of interactive material. It becomes as if the object of existential attachment begins to enact the biological and conceptual makeup of the individual. In this way, the individual prioritizes engaging with the substance of themselves through the objective world in a manner that enables dynamic opposition. Whatever is entailed in the internal realm is the true nature of the substance but lacks the ability to become an interactive opposition.

Existential attachment provides the ability to project the individual onto an object or environment, which then becomes a reciprocal entity embodying aspects of selfhood. Coincidentally, existential attachment generates a data stream that can become redundant, overwhelming, or overly fixated. This can lead one to place themselves in an environment or attach to an object that undermines the wholeness of their personhood, offering only the limited interactions it can provide. In some sense, whenever existential attachment occurs, there is a recalibration of personhood into that domain.

The object receives the existential nature and does not release such unless there is a conscious removal of the bond. The bond is continuously renewed without resolution because the consideration of an already received existential exposition is animated to receive its vitality alongside the vitality of one's innate existence. This becomes a remarkable incident: with the embedding of the existential self into an object, aspect, being, or social construct, there is no return other than a conscious separation from its clause.

We may suspect that more engagement or activity implicating detachment will conclude the bond. Let us unpack both of these premises to determine if they will be productive in their final outcome.

Firstly, the claim that continued engagement allows for separation is similar to a parent-child bond. We may assume the child gains autonomy only after renewed engagement leads to an attachment of such primacy that the only resolution is to form their independence. Contrary to such an assumption is the nature of this choice, in which the child may find a reservoir of unlimited attachment and begin to assume that whatever independence which has been obtained is contrary to the true nature of this attachment and its boundless resources.

We can envision the child following a path to a regressive state in which they were wholly attached to the parent. This presumption is based on a viewpoint taken from the vantage of the parent. According to psyche nature, continued attachment results in an inborn resentment for the loss of personhood through those burdening connections. This causes the psyche to pursue distance and autonomy through a conscious detachment from those objects.

With this notion, the parent projects that happenstance onto the child, assuming they enact the same internal resentment or recognition of their unique makeup. However, this epicenter, assumed to be within the child, is in fact still painstakingly attached to the parent. The parents assume the epicenter will ascend from the burdening attachment, all the while the epicenter is vitalized by its former memory of being attached to the parents. The mistake is the assumption that the child is not fundamentally attached to the parents, leading the parents to believe that there is an epicenter solely secluded from that dynamic.

The same applies to adult attachment. The premise that continued attachment will cause an epicenter to emerge that grants individual independence and separation which is not straightforward. Instead, the attachment only emphasizes the dependency on the object, to which all else becomes diluted, including any epicenter. Therefore, the presumption of the parent, that continued attachment will incur a separation, only produces a less definite epicenter from which to voice resentment.

This would mean that the degree of resentment correlates with the stage of dilution in the epicenter. When resentment is resounding, this may reflect a situation that retains a resolute epicenter, for which every sentimental threat becomes postured. Conversely, a situation of diminished resentment references an already enfeebled epicenter. The burdened individual does not endure a scalable degree of resentment, for the psyche does not retain any sensibility of independence. However, a strong degree of resentment can also denote a disallowance for admissible vulnerabilities, which become incorporated into that weighty notion of independence.

The second premise is that an activity demonstrating separation should be enough to detach the existential connection. When an object or construct receives that existential attachment, the entire psyche undergoes a change such that it falls under the jurisdiction of that entity or construct. For instance, a political construct can be adhered by means of existential significance, to which the individual enacts the entire psyche to participate in the dominion. We cannot perceive the activity of the psyche in order to ascertain the elements that display that dominion, because anything existentially bound becomes inseparable from the subject's internal framework.

Exploring Vulnerabilities and Differentiation in Learning

One can gain significant access by exploring the vulnerabilities of an entity, as the continual downstream of its differentiated parts tends to be never-ending. This critical approach often expenses the wholesome narrative of the entity in favor of preparing for a continual stream of information. The more critical the approach, the more material becomes available for reception. If the entity in question is mostly inexhaustible, this leads to an overwhelming influx of information. The intention behind being critical is to gain access to insights that would otherwise be unobtainable through a more rounded lens. Thus, differentiating the entity can result in significant learning, though it may become problematic if it exceeds certain limits.

While, from the perspective of objective information, the process may seem endlessly revealing, the individual at the receiving end of the material risks losing their individuality in the process. If they lack a background of alternative knowledge, they may result to internalizing the vulnerabilities they are exploring. Because differentiation is not a state of being but a temporary encapsulation of a particular aspect of an entity, one that should not be mistaken for the whole, one may become entangled in that vulnerability. This can become especially problematic if it forms the basis of an entire persona.

For example, a child learns through differentiation of their parental figures and is exposed to those vulnerabilities to extract meaning and understanding. However, without autonomy, the child may only absorb a reservoir of problematic traits from those figures. In typical development, this helps illuminate the nature of the parental figures. But in the absence of individuality, the child may embody those negative aspects as if those traits constituted their entire self.

If the aspect in question is only a fragment of vulnerability, normally offset by the whole of the parental figure, this is not inherently harmful. Yet, if that fragment is embodied as one's entire state of being, it becomes significantly more troubling. This occurs when the knowledge one acquires is so detailed and specific that it becomes their entire theory of knowledge, lacking both a comprehensive picture of the entity and a clear differentiation between themselves and the object of learning.

This dynamic is often less visible in the case of overzealous academics because their inquiry into differentiation, though it involves vulnerabilities, typically occurs at a level abstracted from social embodiment. A developed expertise allows one to approach conceptual vulnerabilities without incurring serious social consequences. Even if those vulnerabilities are internalized, they rarely affect others in ways that provoke concern.

However, an academic who has yet achieved expertise and who engages with subjects of deep social significance may indeed embody these vulnerabilities in problematic ways, creating a social risk. The solution is either to remain learning until one reaches a nuanced grasp of the subject that minimizes those risks or to pursue topics that are less socially charged, thereby mitigating potential fallout either way.

The child, by contrast, lacks the expertise necessary to safely explore learning from their parental figures. Because these figures hold direct social significance, an overzealous attempt to learn from them, especially by approaching their vulnerabilities, could lead to the child's undoing. This is why it is important for the child to offset the inquiry by way of example, to enter into communion with familial relationships of the parental figure, so that they become the habitat of inquiry. In this case, the child approaches the vulnerabilities of their parental figures indirectly, through other social beings. This way, they avoid potential social repercussions that might reprise from being overly receptive, while still gaining insight into their parental figures.

As well, they can reach a state of expertise so that in the return of exploring the parental figures, vulnerabilities will be nuanced and not with problematic social ramifications. The idea is to off-center the social ramifications, so that the inquiry can continue by example or metaphor, but without the ability to overwhelm the social realm, for these relatives do not have the effect in any extensive manner as would the parental figures.

Yet, without the exploration of the differentiation, there can be no learning session with respect to the parental figures, and thus the entity would be considered wholesome at whatever state the previous differentiation occurred. Wholesome entities are dependent on prior differentiation. Consequently, if the last differentiation was fairly general and simplistic, then the wholesome entity standing emulated would also be of that kind.

In this case, however, the individual would be neglecting the subjective separation between themselves and the entity of emulation, resulting in a persistent discontent with the relationship. That discontent is discounted when the emulation does not contain a developed differentiation in response to it. As a result, the individual may realize their discontent as a wholesome emulation, thereby embodying and proceeding with their own discontent.

Being overly critical and approaching with an excess of learning material can cause an individual to become entrenched in the vulnerabilities of the subject or entity of inquiry. By maintaining the standard of social distance, or expertise, one can avoid the social manifestation of the embodiment of those vulnerabilities.

Although the better solution would be to maintain a wholesome settlement, so that even with a critical perspective, one can still perceive the entity as a whole, transforming it from a vulnerability into a forthcoming vitality. We find that achieving balance, maintaining a degree of critical perspective while entering into unison with a wholesome system, points toward the most expansive possibility.

The other choice would be to become an expert, so that the vulnerabilities, even if embodied, would only be upsetting to selfhood and not the social environment. However, it is still the case that one embodied the vulnerabilities, which does endure a social effect even if it not adjudicated. Additionally, avoiding inquiry that lacks social relevance helps prevent forms of differentiation, and thus learning, that hold no real substance for the individual.

However, in the case of a metaphor where the material leads back to a social ramification, such as a child's engagement with a parental figure's relationships, this allows for protection from social manifestation but then again does not protect from embodying vulnerability, as the inquiry involves exploring the vulnerabilities of the entity in question. Therefore, the inquiry consists of following the vulnerability inherent in an entity with social consequences.

When the inquiry is both of social significance and is not based on an expert process of differentiation of that subject, it creates the landscape for the individual to presume that the social learning is the leadership of their conscious system; though this occurs with underdeveloped differentiation, which usually consists of broad sweeps of vulnerabilities. These are the initial vulnerabilities encountered when approaching a new subject.

For instance, if one were not acquainted with mathematics, they might approach addition or subtraction as the method of mathematics. To understand addition, we would need to retreat from the nature of mathematics and numbers as a general system of thought, and instead adopt the stylistic usage of numbers for the procedure of addition. This is a differentiation of numerical systems that is wholesome, to then be utilized in the method of addition. One must lose the general sense of numbers in order to understand addition.

Now, this exposed vulnerability, of disregarding numbers in their natural, subjective manifestation for the sake of the addition process, is far more detrimental for the novice compared to an expert in mathematics. While the novice faces the inevitable downfall in their perception of numbers, the expert is merely identifying a vulnerability in the addition method compared to another method. The embodiment of that vulnerability is not clearly visible in social manifestation, whereas for the novice, the social manifestation is the disregard of a wholesome interpretation of elements, thus becoming critical in many other areas and thereby being exposed to further embodiments of vulnerability. Although the expert is also dealing with this vulnerability, having already gained knowledge of addition, they do not perceive that differentiation as such, but rather connect it to a sequence of knowledge, where the vulnerability lies much further along the spectrum.

Part 3: The Senses

Existential Procurement and Autonomy of the Senses

Approaching the contextual realm from an observation point, where one is immersed without sufficient existential preparation, is the consequence of idle happenstance. The existential procurement is to which personhood is divested through energy consumption of physical movement or conceptual strain. Physical movement is self-explanatory. Conceptual strain is the movement of the psyche in departments which requires a loss of other parts for its continuation.

To procure its movement it necessitates a distinguishing negligence of what is assumed to be stable and interactive ground. We will not go so far as to say that there must be existential availability, for although it includes this, it is not a requirement. Rather the point of the matter is that it alleviates certain parts of the psyche for others, but is only concerning those which are committed for the stability of the entire system. It is the case that there would be a slight experience of existential loss through such movements, but as would someone who is not existentially attached to losses in the psyche to not be existentially vulnerable. They will be fluid towards comfort and discomfort; stability and instability. They are more than willing to adapt the psyche to another realm for exposure and extraction. Because of this characteristic they will not be enticed by an offering of a contextual realm which has as its grievance the promise of non-existential procurement. Already available to physical movements of environments and cultures, the psyche is surely adapted to its own movements from one interactive point to another. While those with the existential attachment to psyche movements, will either be those who are existential available to dramatic changes or will be those who do not perform regular psyche movements. Surely the latter will not physically change environments and societies because that would compel the psyche to those inner movements.

The offering of the contextual realm will be structured to produce an effect of engagement that requires a sensibility of movement without true movement. Without the sensibility of movement there would be no attention for the psyche since it is structured in such a manner. Yet, the movement-offering is only an addendum for the individual which will not require absolute movement. This feat is done through enticing the senses to follow mobility without being mobile. Having the senses enthralled by this conceptual realm will produce coinciding effects. First off will be the stimulation necessary for a sensibility of movement. The second will be an enticement of the senses that will differentiate the senses from overall psyching independence. The idea is to have the senses become enough of an independent experience that it will not have to answer to the overall psyche but will still be enough for sensibility of mobility.

The senses have a manner of being able to follow a realm that is not intertwined with the entire psyche. Its connection to the psyche matter is according to its sensibility of being attached. The only way that the senses understand its attachment to the psyche is when a third referential point in the external realm demonstrates such. It demonstrates the demands of absolute psyche movement upon the senses at large. When there is movement in the psyche, it shall be the case that the sense follows or leads in that direction.

This is because the external point, the social realm or superego, is embedded within the psyche and will be paralleled with the senses. When the senses have its own reference point, it becomes a habitat that is distinguished from the environment and psyche. Although it obviously feeds from and to the psyche, it does so at its own wavelength and is only partially incorporated with rationality.

It may have a system of thinking that will contain a logical continuum but under scrutiny will be identified for lapses of wholeness of personhood. As if this little detail is of immense importance for the overall picture when realistically it is rather a sore point of any relevance in society. The senses only concern themselves with these details not for its consistency with any logical importance but rather to have some sort of connection to the psyche at all. Instead of thinking of these minuscule details as a true point in a rational continuum, it is instead to be looked at as a nuisance which is only an abled in order to facilitate any sort of psychic connection. It is more important that the senses has a psychic connection of sorts to which it vitalizes itself than if it continues on a logical path of any sort. This is why we will find such individuals leap from one point of rationality to another without notice of explanation. The rationality is not there for insight but to maintain psyche and societal connection, and when such is not of interest we will notice a rational gap of extreme measures. If it had its way, logicality would be neglected and full appropriation of the senses will take effect. When this occurs there is an ensuing loss of vitality for the psyche which naturally operates in a sort of rational function and is unable to interact with this bubble of irrationality.

When we discuss the term 'sense,' we are referring to the physical manifestation of bodily and chemical extremities. The senses can be looked at as the reciprocation of bodily and psyche movements. It's a repository or reservoir of the overall picture of personhood and experience with chemical extremes. The connection between the senses and overall personhood is not tightly joined.

If it was the case that the senses were aligned to personhood in full form then it would not be available for its vitalization as its own innate part. It would lose a third party experience and would be a part of systematic function of personhood in which it is not deserving of respite from the rest of it. In other terms, it needs to remain as a feminine backdrop so that their reciprocation between masculine personhood and the senses are separate but dynamical.

One can disrupt the senses as being a differentiated part of personhood and thus will be an experience of low sensitivity and environmentally focused. As we have noted, the psyche is an embedded form within the external environment, so that if the senses are deeply attached to the psyche then it goes to say that the senses are also aligned with the external environment with precision.

This does not mean that the senses have become a true form of the external environment because that would only be possible through the development of the psyche to which we must acclaim a possible degradation through loss of sensitivity. What will be true is that the senses will stride along with the environment without becoming affixed at singular points. As the environment moves in its normal function, so will the senses. At a moment's lapse with heightened anger to the next moment of ecstatic joy. This is the absolute manifestation of an environment which moves as would winds and celestial bodies; never resting upon singular obsessions.

Philosophizing the Senses

We will approach the problem of philosophizing the senses, and by that, we refer to constructing a theory to engage the wholeness of personhood with the substructure of the senses. Because we have noted the stark contrast between the senses in their biological state and their conceptual overlay, to utilize philosophy, a conceptual realm, for the engagement of the senses will only breed a distorted version of their practical manifestation. The senses, although they can be understood through a philosophical lens, as we are attempting to do no less, cannot be approached through that understanding. The conceptual realm cannot arrive at the senses because it is not of the same consistency.

Knowing this, one will understand a philosophical lens on the senses as being a conceptual exercise alone. Once within the sensual realm, all conceptual breath becomes insufficient as a hold for interaction. It may be placed adjacent to the sensual experience to add context to the already given scenario, but it cannot provide the sensual experience nor cause it to move in any specific direction. The moment such an attempt is made, whatever the experience, it becomes a conceptual paradigm that simulates sensual data as if it were the real thing.

The difference between simulated and real sensual data lies in the root of its manifestation. Indications can be observed to notice the simulated effect, as one seems not to progress on the emotional plane, as if every point of understanding does not affect the sensual data but only streamlines a broad flat-line to give the effect that it is cognizant. We can notice this when one actually arrives at sensual data and realizes that the information may be years old, for it has never been accessed in its present form, only having a conceptual overlay that dominates every fair movement, assuming that progress has been made.

A reasonable question may be: to what end does a philosophy of the senses produce any good if we have noted that it will only make it more difficult to accept the non-transient nature of the conceptual realm? The understanding will have multiple benefits, which we will elaborate henceforth.

Firstly, without the understanding of the sensual realm, it may seem arbitrary to engage in its domain while secluded from the conceptual realm. By being aware of its nature, having the necessity of being a realm structured the way it is, one may find it more difficult to disengage from that conceptual understanding when approaching the senses. But it will also produce the adverse benefit of recognizing a domain that deserves its time of day. Without the understanding, it is likely that one will either borrow from unfinished conceptual layers without noticing the loss of sensual data or fail to progress its subtleties. Moreover, to presume that the engagement with the sensual realm is sensual-based, even though it has never left the comfort of the psyche, is a significant oversight.

Secondly, the understanding of the senses will provide insight into the utilization of the conceptual realm to provide context for sensual engagement. Without that insight, one may very well be within the domain of the senses but lack the possible details that would give credence to its substance. Being sensually based, it does not retain the complexity of the conceptual realm, and it can become convoluted, or worse, have an imposed context that may produce a translation guiding the senses to a more rudimentary or animalistic overtone.

If the senses give rise to a threatening sentiment, although we can be sure that a certain form of threat is present while one is inertly within the sensual realm, we still do not know in what manner it is a threat. Moreover, we do not know to what specific aspect of personhood it is a true threat. The sensual data is effective at articulating a true point on a continuum, but not effective at detailing in what context this threat should be treated. Without the placement of a conceptual detail to be picked up by the sensual realm, a context, any context, will be found.

If the sense is a betrayal, it may be assumed that the betrayal renders one an outcast from their domain and thus vulnerable to extreme violence from it, being that they are now a non-entity within it. This will be a context that may be picked up due to the absence of conceptual development to guide the translation. This response will be more relatable to the biological part of the organism, which experiences vulnerability and assumes an existential threat. A conceptual overlay may adjacently attach a context in which societies of inquiry are not in the habit of being violent to everyone outside of their jurisdiction, and the contrary may be true.

The understanding of the senses will help one recognize the importance of utilizing conceptual data alongside sensual data. Still, one can easily fall into the conceptual realm so that, instead of serving as a placeholder for sensual data, it overtakes the whole affair, pragmatic, but not absolute, to the sensual data. This is a normal occurrence because one cannot reside indefinitely in a transitional phase, always available to the in-between of both realms. One must reside either in the sensual realm, making choices that may not be adjacently attached to the conceptual realm, or retain the conceptual realm and fail to notice the true sensual data of their experiences.

Intelligibility in the Senses

The access to the body is through the senses, a loss which will disable the experience of the body. We can even say that there is no experience of the body as it were, but rather a sensory experience which correlates to what we are to call the body. The raw biological entity that is the body may not have any state other than its system of utility, which would not allow for an experience of it. While the senses cannot be simply attributed to the psyche function, because they do correlate to the realness of experience, they are, in fact, associated with being the spokesman of the body.

The senses are the most trusted source of the psyche function, acting as a kind of messenger between the pure psyche and raw biological material. We must admit that there is an element to the senses which is not psyche-based; if they are to act on behalf of both sides. This element is the biological material in activation of itself without psyche assistance. For instance, an element of touch would contain a raw biological aspect which can be stimulated without psychic involvement. The interpretation is nonetheless the product of the psyche's operation, but, as noted, only as an interpretation of an earlier expression.

We must accept, with such a proposition, that there is an element of touch which exists in the biological entity that can be enabled without the actuality of touch. The body can gain a sense of touch because it is not environmentally based. The rawness of its state is accessed through a predecessor to the function of physical touch, through which there is a sensibility, an awareness of the parameters of the organism, that touch is layered upon. The organism seeks to acknowledge its spatial state to know what is intrinsic to it and what is external from it.

Touch evolves from that supposition to become a more elaborate and engineered form of real-time awareness to the happenings that surround the body. We notice that the areas of greater touch sensitivity are more likely to attach to external elements. The hands are the most perplexing parts of the system, as they are a constant accessory to the environment. This creates a problematic confrontation in defining what is external to the self. Thus, the hands are fairly sensitive to grant a sophisticated sentiment of their intrinsic elements compared to those that are temporary and/or external.

The genital area is also fairly sensitive because it is the area that will coalesce with other mating bodies, threatening a loss of the strict parameters of the personhood system. Therefore, the sensitivity of touch makes a clear demarcation between parts that belong to selfhood and those of another organic structure. The more sexual the contact is, the more sensitive is the experience of touch, what is most threatened to the parameters of the system.

If we follow the material that leads to the sensibility of touch, we notice that the body is more concerned with its parameters than with the details of touch. It is aware that something seemingly not part of the body can act upon it by sheer proximity. We can acknowledge this by the way the loss of the sensibility of touch occurs when something previously questioned as external becomes accepted as part of the system, eventually leading to the loss of the need for touch in that context. The sense is only there to determine the parameters of the organism so that it may acknowledge what is internal to its structure and what can be considered environmental. The organism does so because it is interested in facilitating what is internal to the system and is not concerned with facilitating what is not. The system must distinguish what belongs to itself in order for the entire process to continue along the delicate thread of its structure.

The organic structure does not know what is internal to it, which is the vulnerability of any system: it can always be attached to more parts. For its thesis is systemic movement, we can even question the initial sensibility of the body wanting to know its internal structure. We could attribute this to a complex evolution which recognizes that organic matter can only produce a functional system if there is a clear demarcation of what is internal and external. Prior to psychic experience of the body, the organic matter has produced its own sensibility to the identification of its system. But how can a raw system of organic matter identify itself as anything?

We must agree that there is a psyche-like aspect to the organic matter itself from which such sensibility arises. We cannot attribute this to psyche experience as we understand it, but to a forced intelligibility that is a derivative of organic necessity. By the sheer need of organic function, a slight intelligibility is layered; just as the psychic aspect of a modern human came into fruition through organic necessity.

We could say that just as there is a computational system separate from the organic body, there is also a smaller version of such for the body itself. Otherwise, how could an entire psyche development, so different from organic matter, evolve in a system that knows nothing of the sort? Rather, we must say that there is a scalable psyche development at each level of organic matter, of which the final brain is the most separate and the most complex.

However, not to overstate the claim of psyche activity at every level of organic matter, we must admit this is not a psyche experience per se, but rather an intelligibility compelled by the more raw necessities of nature. The psyche known to us can move without much accountability, while raw organic matter has only ascertained a distilled version of intelligibility for a nuanced process of movement that would be detrimental if not entertained. In some sense, the terminology of "biological necessity" refers to how these sub-psyche systems interact.

It is unfair to define these sub-psyche systems as being in correlation to the psyche system we understand. Immediately, we begin our discussion on the conceptual basis of a psyche system that is enlarged and developed beyond organic matter. Therefore, it is not to be called intelligibility in the same vein as true intelligibility, but rather a sensibility of the organic state as it were. Notice that we term the senses as a "sense" of something intelligible, but not intelligible enough to be called more than a sense. The appropriation of the material that manifests as a sense has intelligible backing, but is more so organic material seeking to fulfill its necessities.

The organic matter that reaches a state of sensibility only does so because it is compelled into a corner, to which it must admit some form of intelligibility for further function. When there is no necessity for such emergence, these sensibilities are no longer attended to and are instead utilized through the real psyche system of the mind, all with its own conceptual basis.

Psychic Interpretation and Rhythmic Intelligibility

While sub-psyche sensibilities are biologically grounded, true psychic interpretation adds another layer of complexity. Take hearing, for example: it responds to a deep-rooted biological necessity that demands intelligibility. Just as touch is a proclamation of parameters that define internal and external, hearing differentiates sound originating within the system from sound coming from outside. We might ask: what are these internal sounds that require distinction? They correspond to rhythmic movements we feel. Rhythm is essential for biological processes that must continue uninterrupted. It links each part of the organism into a continuous system, while allowing variation for proper function.

Rhythm must be perceived as a kind of sound, since it cannot be felt by touch (an external mechanism). The "feel" of rhythm is its pulsation, which lets organic matter participate in motion without diverting from the overall system. We can define this movement as an internal reflection of the body moving through its environment, making internal movement a working part of the system.

The movement can only be interpreted through its differentiation from the rest of the system, as a continuous metric. Its continuity and consistency make movement reliable: a system contained within a larger system. Sound, as rhythm, is embedded in the environment and naturally disrupts internal movement. If sound were to override internal systems, it would destabilize the functions required for biological operation. This is why troubling sound environments are immediately distressing to organic matter, not only because of the psyche's distraction, but because the organism must work intensively to distinguish environmental sound from its internal rhythms. In such conditions, all other processes pause while the internal system asserts control to preserve its autonomy.

Sound is, fundamentally, a mark of externality. The rhythm of the internal system does not project itself as sound but remains in a preliminary, pre-sonic state. Similarly, the psyche system generates internal representations of sound to enable thought itself. The psyche process is interpreted through the rhythmic nature of all internal systems, as each thought marks a point on the metric that functions as the pulse of mental movements in the continuum. We notice that with a change in heartbeat, the psyche process changes. Whatever the thought process prior to the heartbeat alteration becomes mislaid in the new psyche state. This is due to the underpinnings of the psyche as an adaptive force for the interpretation of already-existent internal systems. The psyche is a microscope of the rhythm of the internal system; any change in rhythm dramatically affects the psyche process.

The different rhythms of the internal system, for instance, the pulse and breathing, are used for different aspects of the psyche process. The psyche combines all rhythmic measures or relies heavily on one or the other to streamline a coherent dialogue of thought. The interpretation of an existing rhythmic system is based on how one utilizes the psyche system. By following a certain thought formation, attention is accorded to a specific rhythmic function. Compulsive thinking takes hold of a specific rhythmic function, even though there is a requirement to combine systems for appropriating the proper system. By utilizing a single system, the psyche treats the organic matter not as a single organism but rather as parts, interpreting and approaching a single rhythmic system.

The material of those mental movements is less important than the movements themselves. The appropriation of movement into an interpretation of psyche material is the advancement of psyche operation. We could say that the definite pulse placed upon psyche evolution can be interpreted as thought, only that it is organic material unconcerned with content, focusing instead on rhythmic movement.

The psyche, on the other hand, focuses on the material of rhythmic movement. The interpretation process creates a new system of the same rhythmic movement, honing in on a scalable version to identify sub-movements. As it digs into sub-movements, it loses its attachment to the pulsation itself because one cannot entertain a rhythmic measure of a wholly different scale.

The psyche, therefore, becomes available for complexity, it can follow nuance and render intelligible what it is known for. If we follow the lineage of intelligibility, we find it to be a microscopic version of rhythmic pulse, which also cannot be seen under such a lens. Instead, we conjure words such as "complexity," which is the finest scale made possible without losing attention to the material.

The sense of hearing differentiates the rhythmic patterns of water or other external sources from internal rhythms. But before reaching the ear, organic matter follows a sub-psyche pattern that seeks certain interpretations. That process lets the system recognize a subsystem that is both part of and separate from the whole organism. If that subsystem were completely isolated, it would lose vitality; a vital function of organic matter. If it were fully merged, it would risk being subverted within a complex system, losing focus on its differentiated part. While the system can function with a lapse of attention to limbs, it cannot function if it ignores its own pulsation; a core rhythm.

If organic matter lost contact with external rhythms, it would forget what rhythm means. As discussed, rhythmic function is both secluded and included within a larger system that must be learned and unlearned over time. Without outside input to remedy this continual forgetting, the system's individuation gradually erode and it loses a crucial component of organic function.

Thus, external rhythms play a vital role in ongoing learning, which the internal system constantly forgets. Hearing is the bridge that allows rhythmic function to transfer from the environment to the internal apparatus. Although it can overwhelm the system, since the internal system relies on consistency and simplicity, hearing also helps the system distinguish external rhythms from its own. When rhythmic input arrives by other means (e.g., touch or vibration), the internal apparatus cannot easily separate external from internal sources. Still, because rhythmic function transferred without hearing lacks complex sound modulations, it does not threaten to disrupt the internal system but rather helps regulate it.

Sound, being rich in sub-rhythms, can unsettle the organism. Yet it is not distressing to the psyche, which mirrors sound; both operate through micro-rhythmic processing that supports detailed interpretation and the formation of complexity. Although this might seem to confine intelligibility to complex rhythmic functions, no psychic experience could exist without the foundational advancement of organic matter.

Therefore, regardless of sound complexity or intelligibility, it remains an elevated form of rhythm. Its vulnerability lies in over-focus on microscopic details, ignoring rhythm's performance at the normal, pulsatile level. The content of intelligibility is never more important than its structure; or, put another way, knowledge is never as important as wisdom. A database of knowledge (various microscopic perspectives on rhythms) only matters if it supports a full rhythmic integration aligned with true, real-time movement.

From this perspective, something is intelligible if its rhythmic pulse can be traced from a microscopic representation back to real-time pulsation. Microscopic data is legible only if we see that movement as part of the normal organic flow. By contrast, something is unintelligible when the microscopic image is so dense or unpredictable that it reveals no clear path to real-time rhythms.

The value of content lies in the scale on which its rhythm is perceived. The central idea: content *exists to serve* structure. Consider "the sun rises in the morning." The sun itself carries no inherent content; its rising allows certain concerns to emerge. Say instead, "a star rises on a distant planet." The meaningful content is somewhere. Remove somewhere, rising, or *star*, and universal concepts—movement, celestial form, time, and environmental influence, collapse.

Following these structures, say, "rising", we see it serves a more basic concept: movement away from the body in an upward direction. That leads to spatial awareness of top and bottom, and of movement in general. "Celestial bodies" serve the idea of "ground," experienced when other grounds are available. "Ground" serves the concept of the body, experienced through touch. The body, in turn, serves its spatial habitat as an organism, which then allows derivative touch rather than movement. The intellectual idea of "celestial body" is not a product of rhythmic function, but of sub-psyche intelligibility that recognizes the body's interior against the external world.

Anything that mirrors one's conceptualization of the organism, person, celestial body, ground, derives from biological intelligibility, not from the rhythmic function of ordinary psychic dialogue. Thus, there will always be an impulse toward intelligibility that emphasizes closeness to the organic structure's sub-psyche system.

The sub-psyche benefits from being limited in intellectual scope yet more directly connected to organic matter. This is why it is hard to deceive the senses: they retain an intelligibility rooted in biological reality. Although we can manipulate the senses, we do so not through the senses themselves, but through the psyche's interpretation of them. For example, if there is a sense of touch to a part of the body that is not the cause of external pressure nor internal mechanisms, we can ascribe such to psyche manipulation of the overall interpretation of all senses. We can acknowledge this by paying attention to the streaming of thought that pertains to that sensibility of touch, to notice that it is psyche-based and not found in the biological entity. Distinctions such as specificity of the point of touch since the overall psyche interpretation does not have the ability to manipulate a specific point, but rather can cover an overall area of a certain circumference, are important. Specificity of touch can only be manifested from the biological entity itself, because it does not have the ability to entertain intelligibility that is not pertaining to biological necessity itself.

Therefore, the psyche's ability to manipulate the senses is only available when the senses' data is not protected for its own right, so that visual paranoia is only apt in personhood that does not differentiate visualization that is biologically founded, in stark contrast to interpretation measures of the psyche experience. The closer one gets to the data material of the senses as it were to manifest in genuine form, the less able the psyche will be to approach the senses or the interpretation of the senses with its own parameters of intelligibility.

The fault of sub-psyche systems is that they are enveloped by the absolute psyche system and can be forgotten for their material substance. Besides the mentionable manipulation of the psyche which is now available to territorial claim, it is also the loss of utilization of the senses for applicable data mining that pertains to testimonial presence. The psyche, while being a potent force of the human condition, is faulted in being able to present fabricated, imaginative, or other forms of intelligibility that do not make a great case for the testimony of reality as it were in most absoluteness. The domain for such availability is only found in the senses' data stream, which does not even have the ability to fabricate its reception nor be at the behest of wrongful interpretation, distinguishing when the material manifests from its domain and is not subjugated through overall psyche expansion.

We will differentiate by following the visual material that manifests naturally and the secondary interpretation. There are two images to each sight: one is the immediate sensation of the transfer of light into the inner domain of organic matter, and the other is the interpretation of such through another image. The first image is similar to when seeing something for the first time or entertaining a sight for the first time, in which the material is so raw or new that there's an inability of psyche interpretation to follow or project its framework upon it. By default, the reception of material is true to its nature and can be called a sub-psyche stream.

However, it is the case that all visual material contains or retains that initial visualization as a new image. It is only covered by the preeminent psyche material that has already fortuned the fate of that visual sentiment. To access the initial visualization, what must first occur is a renunciation of the psyche and a recognition of the image as it is, prior to and independent of mental stipulations. There's no real mental data to the sight, since we are used to frameworks that are built in the psychic department that give meaning to imagery. This visualization is just the appropriation of distinguishing aspects of color and light that further into the inner sanctum of the organic structure. The material of the image only matters so much as the organic structure finds interest in that visualization.

This involves either a spatial recognition of the internal system in contrast to external imagery, or a vitalization of the realness within an external image, affirming its equivalence to the internal mode of operation. The second point is crucial, as the organic structure itself does not acknowledge its own vitalization; vitalization is a concept that belongs to a reality framework encompassing all external realms to the fullest extent.

Vitalization is closely associated with external expansion and cannot be an internal manifestation by virtue of a thing siphoned off from what is a known-reality or possible reality. For a child, whose known or possible reality extends only slightly beyond their immediate domestic environment, the external world remains inaccessible. Their vitalization is tied to the full domestication of their home space, but they cannot yet conceive of the external realm as a possible reality framework for their internal experience.

While mature adults understand a further degree of the conceivable external realm, they will only gain vitalization as much as the external realm is explored according to the limits of the psyche's envisioning of a horizon. That horizon does not have a limit, to which there is a certain maturity in that which may surpass a socially acceptable horizon, such that they will not find vitalization unless they explore what has been included into their apparatus as an imaginable external realm.

142

Emblematic Mapping and Embodiment of Emotion

The Distancing–Embracing model, as articulated by Menninghaus et al. (2017), proposes that art allows for a safe interaction with negative emotions by providing psychological distance.v This estrangement prevents overwhelming distress and enables a controlled engagement with fear, anxiety, or anger. However, while this model acknowledges a way to process emotions from a safe space, we should argue for a more thorough analysis. The horror film or the cathartic experience is not simply a safe way to interact with emotion, it is itself the ability to engage with emotion.

What remains locked within the psyche is not simply an undefined or repressed emotion; rather, it is not a full emotion whatsoever because it lacks a perceptual landscape. It lacks sociality, linguistic detail, and compartmentalization, the very aspects that define an emotion as an experiential reality. One does not simply confront their emotions; rather, emotions must be mapped onto an external experience in order to exist as something tangible.

This is why horror, Halloween, or other symbolic rituals allow for anxiety to take form in the external world. When we embody fear, anger, or dread in a perceptual environment, we create a reality where these emotions can be engaged rather than remaining laden within the psyche. Psychology, by contrast, does not always achieve this because it tends to confront emotions contained by the psyche itself rather than externalizing them in a structured, emblematic form.

This is where Jungian archetypal theory approaches something approximating our argument: emotions do not simply reside within, they must be projected outward, taking form in myth, symbol, and embodied ritual. vi Without external mapping, anxiety or anger cannot be synthesized with the unconscious, because there is no perceptual structure that allows for it.

In prehistoric societies, this was achieved naturally. The cultural tribe would embody horror and fear through ritual, externalizing these emotions into the social sphere. Similarly, anger was given expression through structured external representations. With the classical Greeks internal mechanisms took over this charge. While the classical Greeks still recognized the fictional reality of myth and tragedy, they did not reduce emotional experience solely to an internal process. Instead, they understood that the psyche itself cannot function appropriately without mapping emotions onto an external, perceptual experience.

This process is evident in hierarchical, elitist cultures, where social structures provide clear external expressions of the internal psyche. Rivalries are not just psychological, they are fully embodied experiences. Hatred, resentment, and other antagonisms are mapped onto social hierarchies, not necessarily to produce real conflict, but to allow for an interaction with the mechanisms of the psyche that require rivalry and differentiation. When external rivalry is absent, the psyche remains undifferentiated. There is a false sense of unity, but no real dynamic interplay. The psyche does not fully learn its own structure because the emotions remain internalized rather than engaged in a structured realm.

The critique of elitist culture is that it appears to be a retracement of antiquated social divisions. These structures do not exist chastely for the sake of hierarchy, they serve as a means of expression, almost like a dance, where social antagonisms play out in a way that allows people to interact with their own psyche. It would be mistake in assuming that internal psychological processes can function independently of external mappings.

Without a perceptual environment that allows anxiety, anger, or rivalry to take form, these emotions remain vague, undefined sensations rather than experiences. In societies lacking emblematic expressions of rivalry, such as certain indigenous cultures with no structured external conflicts beyond direct social interactions, anger remains general and undirected. There is no reality or framework for differentiation, making the emotion far less defined than it would be in a perceptually structured environment. In contrast, when an emotion is given form, through horror, myth, social hierarchy, or ritual, it is no longer an abstract sensation.

Thus, while the Distancing–Embracing model correctly identifies a safe way to interact with negative emotions, it underestimates the necessity of external mapping. The psyche does not simply experience emotion; it requires emblematic mapping to form an actual emotional landscape. The absence of this externalization leads to an undifferentiated emotional state, while structured external experiences provide the necessary framework for emotions to become fully realized and consciously processed.

Emotionative Immediacy in Embodiment

External embodiment can be understood in two fundamental ways: emotionative immediacy and emotional mapping. Emotionative immediacy allows for the raw expression of emotion without structural intervention, while emotional mapping organizes and refines emotion through artistic composition.

A key distinction exists between these two orientations is that one involves the recipient allowing emotion to exist as it is, while the other involves creating something new by mapping emotion into a structured form. The former is about experiencing emotion intensely, while the latter is about reconfiguring it into something new through artistic design.

Emotionative immediacy allows for direct emotional influx but does not define it for further conversation. In contrast, emotional mapping involves a process that forces differentiated dynamics between art forms, leading to a changed emotional experience rather than simply mirroring the original feeling.

An interesting paradox emerges with emotional mapping. While it offers sophistication and transformation, it also distances the recipient from the authentic experience of emotion. The structure imposed by emotional mapping means the experience does not truly belong to the recipient, but rather to the constructed framework of that perceptual embodiment. The emotional experience conveyed through the mapping process belongs to the social creation, not to the immediate, raw emotion itself.

Emotional mapping is often described as more cerebral, while emotionative immediacy is considered more primal. Emotional mapping creates a narrative intervention, reshaping emotion, while emotionative immediacy mirrors reality without reshaping it. This distinction raises the question of whether sociality serves as a mirror or as a reframing device. These two approaches define how emotion is processed, either as a raw presence or as designed experience.

Perception and the Boundaries of Selfhood

Perception can be considered prevalent as the access point through which one sets boundaries between selfhood in its experience of itself and the external world with which selfhood interacts from which it is wholly separate. At the extreme end of perception, or its possibility, is the inclusion of every possible external form integrated as if it were selfhood, even extending into elements perceived through a far stretch of imagination.

Schizophrenics may still require certain geometrical forms within the perceptual realm to construct their imagery. First and foremost, there is this external "box" that can now be filled with imaginary elements, or repainted, or reimagined. It may be the case that without the geometrical form to manipulate perception, for perception by its default nature is the integration of external form, whatever the range of imaginatory elements, a certain foundational agreement with the external realm is required to become integrated with the imaginatory realm.

There is a pact made between the psyche and perception whereby each offsets the other, so that a conclusive interpretation of the external form is formatted in a manner beneficial to the paradoxical relationship: serving the internal realm and its disagreement with external forms, and external form for its role as a catalyst for what is beyond, or rather beneath, the processes of the psyche. "Beneath" in the sense that whatever is the basis of the psyche in its most accessible state exists only upon the foundation of what is outside of it, and thus cannot be seen by its own realm. "Beyond" refers to the possibility of the psyche's happenstance degenerating to a point where only what is beyond is the efficacious realm. Thus, the first is conciliatory to birth, a state before any state exists, and the latter is the realm of what would be without the state of being.

Those who are inclined toward the notion of being without the state of being accept, and almost loathe, the state of non-existence. This is not non-existence in its conclusion, where no access is possible, even for what lies beyond. Rather, it is the specific moment of death, where there remains just enough of a state of being to simultaneously be without being and still be available to what is beyond. Such individuals will utilize perception as a tool to see external forms without little overlay from the psyche. For they already endure a state where *being* and the psyche's happenstance cease to exist.

In the case of those who view what is external to selfhood as the foundational element of the psyche, preceding the psyche, that is, they will view the perceptual realm as analogous to the state of birth, which enters into the notion of a void upon which birth is laid. In this way, external form becomes the applicable aspect of one's psyche that is not consciously agreed to exist, or the unconscious, which takes the place of external form as the mechanism of birth, the shadow of conscious states of mind. This is the area where psychology takes hold: the utilization of perception in its realization of the unconscious realm, where the foundational elements of current conscious experience now become the treaty with the external form, resulting in dread or love, depending on those foundational elements. In some sense, we see the counterbalance to psychology in the utilization of the perceptual process as it relates to the notion of death, or the moment just before death, into which courage and other traits aligned with that criteria are not explored within psychology, and remain at the opposing end of that spectrum.

Psychology ends its analysis where the psyche's happenstance is no longer overlaid upon the external realm, and symptoms no longer arise because of it. Instead, it enters into the realm of the ending of being, where the entire spectrum from unconscious to conscious experience is rendered futile, and only the state of being that ends itself, and begins what lies beyond it, remains. Another trait psychology does not uncover is glory, which is a form of experience in that very moment between the end of being and what lies beyond. A third trait psychology cannot include is cruelty, which is the process of the periphery receiving stimulation from one's delineation of being; also the manner by which one experiences oneself in that very state. Therefore, the traits of courage, glory, and cruelty, in their various forms, are excluded from the realm of psychology. For any symptom, the answer could be courage, glory, or cruelty, and the discourse stops.

This is why fear or anxiety is limited to a certain perceptual access, even if far-fetched, so that it brings the foundational layer into the setting. One may note the difference between anxiety and the impending dread of anxiety: the latter is simply the awaiting of imaginatory elements within the psyche's happenstance to be placed upon a perceptual form; elements which have not yet found a geometrical external portal to embody that anxiety. Thus, it waits to place that imagery, so that full-form perception for a full-form anxiety can become actualized.

In this way, we understand the perceptual realm as not only a mediator between external forms and internal forms but also the mechanism through which one defines one's own boundaries in deference to what is external; in the same manner as the external in its interpretive format.

One may experience a complicated psyche happenstance or discombobulation but remain affixed to the inner domain, rather than finding an external perceptual experience to which that energy may be applied. Although it may seem causal for the perceptual experience to reimagine the internal world upon the external form, this is not the conclusion if one recognizes, at a high level, the perceptual separation from the psyche's happenstance and its interpretive elements. In this way, the boundary of the psyche is enforced by its very application of that boundary, rendering it unable to apply a high degree of imaginatory overlay upon perceptual experience.

This would be beneficial in cases where it would be more than natural to apply imaginatory elements, such as in the presence of threatening external forms, so that one would see the external form as it truly is, not as it may often pronounce itself. In this way, natural dread is avoided. However, this may counterbalance the beneficial effect of allowing the psyche's happenstance and imagery to overlay external forms, only because it may be necessary to avoid the conclusion of that dread. For instance, in the noticeable forms of detriment within a relationship, if one avoids the imagery overlay that places unusual dread upon what appears to be an imminent detriment, one may retrofit their approach to avoid an outcome which, once realized, is too late for an amicable solution.

On the other side, we encounter the constant overlay of psyche happenstance or imagery upon perceptual forms, which can lead to extreme reinterpretations of perceptual forms that are otherwise simplistic and unambiguous. This is where one may become highly anxious or prematurely conclusive about perceptual forms lacking sufficient evidence to support such imagery. Furthermore, not all imagery is directly connected to perceptual form; rather, it is often the happenstance of the psyche at that very moment, attaching itself to whatever perceptual form is present in order to project that imagery, thus using perception as a facilitator of psyche happenstance onto the external realm, rather than its more typical function of bringing external forms into the psyche as raw external happenstance.

Perception, Psyche, and Foundations of Psychological Discourse

We hold within us a notion aligned with Freud's initial remarks on the libidinal drive and the death drive, remarks which, although originally framed as the conflicting state in which the psyche resides, may be understood as the conflict between the conscious and unconscious realms; and a psychic process that entirely overlooks its own development.vii Only in accordance with perception does one have the axis of one's conscious or subconscious roles. We require geometrical forms in the external front to give rise to all symptoms, because it is the perceptual realm that brings actualization to the state of one's mind. Everything beyond that can either be viewed as foundational to the conscious or subconscious; or arbitrary, for being does have the ability to see beyond it by its very own delineation in the moment of degeneration or death.

If we take Roman or Greek philosophy, surely the traits that we've mentioned before are going to be centered, because of the manner in which they viewed perception: not as something that reveals the conscious and subconscious realms or the foundation of being, but rather as something that includes these realms while going beyond them. Thus, it does not transform the perceptual realm but is rather the very thing that provides the death wish, through which one sees beyond.

Contrary to regular discourse, in which it is assumed that the Romans or Greeks were stronger in their disposition and thus able to follow these traits, traits ignored by modern psychology, it is rather the case that it is simply the extreme of psychology that assumes these traits cannot be developed. To acknowledge them would require delineating the entire process of psychology, especially given its evidential format of truth. We do not have to go far to notice the difference, especially in indigenous or developing populations, where these archaic usages of traits, and particularly the way they view perception as what lies beyond and thus as a culmination, show that they are not, in effect, subject to the detriment of psychology and its very symptoms.

Especially if we consider that these symptoms are not necessarily expressions of all considerations, but rather of a specific perspective on being itself, to which others are available, particularly in the viewing of personhood as something beyond itself. We will always notice that disparity in indigenous or developing populations, where psychological symptoms may be observed if extracted, because there is a sensibility to the foundation of personhood. Still, these symptoms do not plague the individual or its encompassing society due to this perceptual difference. It is only when there is influence or effect, when they are thus propelled to adopt the perception of the psyche's happenstance and foundation, that they become part of the inclusion into the psychological format.

Interaction, Embodiment, and Limits of Social Normativity

Contrast is essential in the modality of engagement and interactivity. Mere likeness results in replication, offering nothing new, while wholehearted distinctiveness, without reference, becomes valueless for meaningful engagement. The only viable path to both integration and distinction is through contrast.

As Rietveld (2008) observes:

"Directed discontent and, more generally, being moved to improve, emphasize the noteworthy combination of object-directed responsiveness, context sensitivity, emotion, and normative instinct that is characteristic of skillful unreflective action."[viii]

Improvement is not generally a form of attenuation, at least in the regular case. Although the craftsman may contrast to improve as a formal sequence, this is not necessarily a psychological endeavor. From the perspective of the psyche, the craftsman's sole objective is interaction, and through experience, they come to determine that the most effective means of engagement is through contrast. Thus, one is compelled to improve by virtue of interaction, rather than the reverse.

The craftsman is no different. Interaction is their aim. We may observe that those who are below average do not meet the standard of improvement, while those who engage consistently will inevitably improve in relation to the object of concern. The improvement might not garner market appreciation, but through contrasting some element, which is then adhered to the object for realignment, it becomes imprinted as such.

Interaction, Growth, and Systems

This can be seen in the universal application of the concept "growth," particularly in moral and psychological development, where it connotes aliveness rather than serving as a staging ground for development or stagnation. In other fields, like finance, growth is equated with stability, while a lack of growth signifies failure.

We take this for granted, rejecting stability as a medium and not recognizing it as the formation of a system. This is because the true inquiry is one of interaction. In finance: "Has the company adequately interacted with market events?" In moral growth: "Has the person properly attended to their existential state?" And in psychology: "Has the individual interacted with their process of being, by stimulating the general themes that control their psyche's happenstance?"

Although contrast is the determinant for interaction, it remains unsolicited until it arises from a preliminary framework within a more adequate system. A non-craftsman who engages an object, contrasts it, and dictates its improvement may have interacted with it, but only through a system lacking a more elaborate form of interaction.

Only through the constant modality of interaction does the craftsman gain proprietary knowledge. Though some may assume this knowledge is tradition, this is not always the case. The non-craftsman has only just begun the process of interaction; thus, the act of contrasting does not emerge from a sufficiently developed preliminary state. For contrast to be meaningful, a system must already be in place, just as a composite picture can only display contrast once it functions as a unified composition.

Contrast vs. Negation

Thus, contrast is only as performative as its underlying composition. In certain situations, contrast may be mistaken for negativity. If we follow the etymology of the word, where the objective is to negate from a preliminary composition, we find concrete footing. There must be a system from which to negate. But such a composition might not seek to include the object or character of inquiry. Instead, it may preclude contrast before engagement.

Thus, the difference between contrast and negation is that the former has already performed the process of interaction and inclusion, to which a contrast is empowered so as to style distinct entities and consequently a development of interaction concludes with more than it started with. However, in the latter case, negation utilizes the modality of contrast but does so before even broaching on interaction or inclusion, almost like recognizing the entity enough to make out form, but just when that form was to be included into one's system, it is precluded with negation in the form of contrast; as if it already performed the deed of existential vulnerability thru engagement and now has reached the other side.

In the case of social relations, many a time the two may be confused, and those who contrast are assumed to negate, even as though this is the only manner of genuine interaction. Without such, it would be *validation* to which individual happenstance is already sufficient of a system to validate itself without sociality, and rather domestication would perform that process.

"This central role of affective behavior also sheds light on the lived experience of normative constraint; the much-neglected phenomenon of lived normativity." (Rietveld)

For Rietveld, he affirms that affective behavior, or in our terms, contrast, is the generation of a social normality to which one seeks to follow a normal function. However, sociality, although it proposes normal function, is by no means the concern of all sociality, but only those who are interested in its interaction.

Sociality and normative function are the forms a social system may take. One can either integrate into such systems or not, just as one can join a family system and adopt its norms, which will differ from another's.

Rietveld elaborates:

"The engaged expert's expressive behavior is internally related to the normative adequacy of the object on which she is working. Therefore, we can describe the state of the whole system made up by the expert directed at the object in its context equally well by referring to, for instance, the present state of the object in the world (not yet correct, but being improved), to the behavior of the expert (she is improving the object), to the expression on her face (dissatisfied with the object), or to her first-person experience ('I am still not content with it')." (Rietveld)

"The state of the whole system directed at the object," which can be rearticulated in our manner, is that this system is the psychological formation of the prior engagements with this object and its associations, but Rietveld deviates. Instead, for him, the context is either the state of the object in the world, self-consciousness in concern with the object, or first-person embodiment.

Finally, he concludes, "As such, the lived normativity of being moved to improve by the object is publicly expressed." Thereby forming his argument that lived normativity is part of a larger social system, when two realms are distinct psychological processes.

Embodiment vs. Social Norms

We could see from his observation that the context must either be the social state of the object or the social experience of the individual in regards to the object, which are both criteria of a broader social system; as if the craftsman can only enjoin in formation based on a social normativity.

For him, normativity is merely a function of social norms, but it can remain universal if we consider *normality* as a framework that accommodates various definitions. There is the possibility of a craftsman who utilizes the social market or social affection in their trade, but that is not the normative function of craftsmanship. Using the evidence of the tradition of all these trades is only the contextual framework of craftsmanship, not the social experience of direct work.

We would even venture to state that the craftsman who has as his normativity the state of the object for the world or for selfhood is one who does not interact with the object, and the directed discontent is nonexistent. If for the state of selfhood, why find discontent with selfhood which is embodied in the object, if at any event they could validate a perfected function of selfhood?

"That very contrast which delineates selfhood does imply a degradation of certain personae within craftsmanship, and perhaps even of one who seeks to delineate selfhood, yet it in no way reflects the natural function of craftsmanship itself. One can theoretically embody whatever object, become unified, and then follow with contrast, but it would seem like a moral problem rather than procedure. In the other case, where one inquires on "the state of the object in the world," this is another irregular state of a craftsman, who focuses on market attention while attenuating the object. Almost as if he came from the market to fashion the role of craftsmanship rather than to perform in its natural procedure.

Only one who precludes the interaction of the object in controlling with broad sociality and tradition will have such an outlook. In this case, they are embodied not in the object, for the criteria of judgment is based on sociality, the realm they are most concerned with. The object is only a thoroughfare to which one can partake in the interaction of sociality. In regular procedure, sociality does not exist, unless we mean the sociality of one's psyche. The object is only a thoroughfare to which one can partake in the interaction of sociality.

Community, Perception, and Psyche Process

The community-centric process that adheres to construct, in this case, craftsmanship, is of no consequence to regular procedure and direct work. They are the archive to which one gains knowledge, not for interaction, for one cannot transfer the experience of interaction by any means but must enable their own development of such.

This knowledge contributes to a certain criteria, but it does not explicitly appear in the craftsman's work. The craftsman knows what to do and what not to do, not because of the community they belong to, as though sociality were a prerequisite for this function, but because community is the only medium through which functional knowledge is transmitted and generated. There could be the craftsman that is community-centric, but then in that case would be interacting with the object based on regulating their state within the community and not in the role or trade of craftsmanship.

There should be no reason to include sociality in perception and its processes, for sociality is a discipline and nothing more in terms of psyche process. One perceives the object despite sociality, and that perception can be developed through knowledge which happens to require sociality but is not dependent upon it. Once we agree that the object has entered the psyche by way of perception, we can only follow the process of either integration in its normal function or negation as a psyche construct that disallows that process.

If integration is the modality, then embodiment is forthcoming and the object and person become unified; this is when one can employ a psyche process that contrasts to the material, to which it becomes distinct entities of material but is performative to engage between the two. At its culmination, contrast provides the necessary teaching and can then be set aside from ongoing integration. Sociality should be considered only for its intrinsic role in the discipline of knowledge, namely, the teaching of psychic tools that can be learned and unlearned, but it is never the formative function of the psyche process.

Embodiment and the Learning Psyche

Hobson emphasizes sociality as key to psychic development:

"The child starts out by reacting to the world in her own terms...She finds a toy alluring, for example. She then perceives her mother relating to that toy with disgust or fear. According to the mother's reaction, the toy is not so alluring. What then happens is that the toy loses its appeal for the child herself. Its meaning has changed because of what it means to someone else...The discovery is a discovery in action and feeling, rather than a discovery in thought." *(Hobson, 1993)*[ix]

We are offered to conclude from Hobson that sociality was the correct performance of learning for the child, while we did not question the onset of that sociality. Surely the sociality of a child to their mother is greater than the affection of a toy, so that a single embodiment, that of child and mother, is teaching another, that of child and toy.

However, the reason the child has affection for their mother is because of an embodiment that did occur, to which at a preliminary stage, whether chronically or phenomenologically, the child did not embody the mother as an object. Rather, the child began from a process of interaction, where such was enabled by perception without choice.

Perception is the data of reception from outward realms that breaches the psyche without control, and it is this disruption that is the cause of any further premise. The disruption causes the psyche to split into two parts: one consisting of receptive material, and the other representing a preliminary state that precedes it, along with distinct parameters that cannot be altered by incoming data.

This is the state of embodiment, which if we looked microscopically, would find distinct entities that are unified under a third formation of the psyche which is tasked with that mediation. Then the child can contrast, which is the inherent recognition of the mediation that appears unified to which one is a substrate of preliminary data and the other of perception's disruption. In this case, the material is contrasted to which learning is made possible. If, as Hobson claims, is correct, one would never be able to separate from their mother, as if the mother is part of the child's psyche rather than perceptual material like any other.

[i] Claude Lévi-Strauss, *Tristes Tropiques* (1962 [1955]).

[ii] Claude Lévi-Strauss, *Tristes Tropiques* (1962 [1955]).

[iii] Abraham H. Maslow. (1943) *A Theory of Human Motivation.* Psychological Review.

[iv] Diamond, M. (2023). *Sexual behavior in Pre-contact Hawai'i: A Sexological Ethnography.* Journal of Sex Research.

[v] Menninghaus, W., Wagner, V., Hanich, J., Wassiliwizky, E., Jacobsen, T., & Koelsch, S. (2017). *The Distancing–Embracing Model of the Enjoyment of Negative Emotions in Art Reception.* Behavioral and Brain Sciences, 40.

[vi] Jung, C. G. (1959). *The Archetypes and the Collective Unconscious.*

[vii] Freud, Sigmund. (1920) *Beyond the Pleasure Principle.*

[viii] Rietveld, E. (2008). *Situated normativity: The Normative Aspect of Embodied Cognition in Unreflective Action.* Mind.

[ix] Hobson, R. P. (1993). *The Emotional Origins of Social Understanding.* Philosophical Psychology.